MERRY CHRISTMAS!

D0771991

RENEWALMENT-
THRIVING IN RETIREMENT

RENEWALMENT–
THRIVING IN RETIREMENT

Building on a Rock-Solid Foundation
of Biblical Principles

BRUCE A. FEAR

XULON PRESS

Xulon Press
2301 Lucien Way #415
Maitland, FL 32751
407.339.4217
www.xulonpress.com

Paperback ISBN-13: 978-1-66284-853-7
Ebook ISBN-13: 978-1-66284-854-4

TABLE OF CONTENTS

Why People Retire
Why People Don't Retire
Why People are Disillusioned
Personal Story
Path Forward

Biblical View of Work
Biblical View of a Life of Leisure and Laziness
Biblical View of the Christian Lifestyle
Biblical View of Vocation (Calling)
Biblical View of Wise Financial Principles
Biblical View of Retirement
Path Forward and Personal Experience
Summary

The Habits Loop
God Owns it All
The Christian Lifestyle
    Provision
    Contentment

ACKNOWLEDGEMENTS

As a reluctant author, I'm indebted to those who encouraged me to start and continue to push forward, particularly Wally Peterson, Tim McCain, Jim Stover, and Doug Slaybaugh. Thank you.

I'm thankful for conversations with and the writings of fellow followers of Jesus like Ron Blue, Dr. Larry Lindsay, and our friends at Ron Blue Institute and Kingdom Advisors have helped shape my thinking and application. The foundation of this work is, hopefully, built on the inspired Word of God through scripture and the Holy Spirit. Thank you.

I'm also thankful for the career/vocation experiences I've had over the last few decades and continue to have. These experiences helped shape the messages in this book as they were formulated and refined, helping me gain clarity on the why, the what, and the how of thriving in retirement. There are numerous people - too many to name - who I've had the honor of walking alongside as we continue to learn. This includes family, friends, peers, and/or coaching clients. Thank you.

I also have a deep appreciation to those who read the manuscript and provided me with valuable insights and Kayla Fear who designed the graphics.

I'm indebted to Nicole Pilgrim. Nicole did the editing and proofreading of this book, along with challenging me on language, flow, and structure. Without her expertise and encouragement, the content would not have turned into a book. Thank you.

I also owe a shoot out to Mark Holt, Mountain Sage Consulting, Estes Park, CO. Mark was the first one I heard use the word Renewalment. Thank you for your insights, Mark.

Without the love and encouragement of my wife Bonnie, our three children, their spouses, and of course our grandchildren, this book would have never been written and I wouldn't be thriving in Renewalment (retirement). I love you and there's no one I'd rather be on this journey with. Thank you.

Thank you for reading this book. My prayer is that you will find a few nuggets that you can grab ahold of and implement as you live into a life of peace, provision, contentment, and enjoyment on the rock-solid word of God.

INTRODUCTION

WOULDN'T YOU AGREE that retirement is an important life transition? It's a phase of life that we must plan for, and simply can't afford to just let it happen. It's important to take the time to reflect, discern, and plan for this phase of life. Anyone can thrive in retirement with a little planning. Because it is such an important phase of life, it deserves your attention!

How do you react when you think about your retirement years? Are you anxious? Have you ever asked yourself any of the following questions as you think about retirement?

- What will I do in retirement?
- Can I really engage in a hobby seven days a week for the next twenty to thirty years?
- What if I run out of money?
- How much money do I need in order to retire?
- How do I enjoy - even thrive - in retirement?
- What will my purpose be in retirement? Will it be fulfilling?
- What will I do all day long and what will matter to me?
- What will my identity be? How will I be useful?
- What would it mean to become irrelevant when I retire?
- How will my spouse and I survive all that time together?

There's a decent chance you've at least wondered about the above questions. Do they create anxiety? Are you trying to ignore them, hoping they'll go away? Unfortunately, they will not go away and they certainly won't answer themselves.

To thrive in retirement, it's important to intentionally ask and answer these and other questions unique to you.

While the above questions are important, my experience and belief is that the following questions are even more important to ask and answer if you desire to thrive in retirement:

- What does the Bible have to say about retirement?
- What guidance does the Bible give me? Are there key principles to follow?
- What does the Bible say about work and a life of leisure?
- What does the Bible say about living a Christ-like lifestyle?
- What does the Bible say about money?
- Where will I find my identity and purpose in retirement?
- With Jesus as my best friend, what might retirement look like?
- What the heck is "Renewalment" and why is it important?

Together we'll discuss the above questions to help guide you in developing a rock-solid foundation on which to live your retirement years. This foundation will help you thrive in retirement! I'll give you the path to follow, but only you can work through the questions and answer them for your unique situation and personal goals for retirement. Take the time to be intentional when planning, and as your guide, I'll help you:

- Explore why most people become disillusioned in retirement and how to avoid that outcome.
- Reframe and clarify your perspective of retirement.
- Gain clarity of your identity, core values, purpose, and vocation in relation to your retirement.
- Identify what is "enough" for you financially, as well as your retirement income approach and perspective.
- Discern and clarify the unity of your retirement structure in order to embrace the flexible rhythm of your new life.
- Define "Renewalment" and how it differs from the typical worldview of retirement.
- Design your Renewalment game plan for thriving in this new phase of life, not just surviving.

You're much more likely to get to your desired destination if you're intentional about where you're headed. With a little intentionality and structure, anyone can thrive in retirement.

The intention of this book is to help you find clarity and a path forward for living a life of provision, as well as contentment and enjoyment. This will enable you to provide for your family with a healthy mix of margin. As a result, you'll find yourself being content with what God has entrusted to you. You will live "guilt free" because you can confidently multiply what you steward for His glory, and simply enjoy what God has blessed you with.

A Few Personal Insights About Renewalment

I've observed a significant number of individuals and couples who seem to be thriving as they strive for the cultural version of retirement. However, when they finally reach their retirement years, the cracks in this approach are exposed and they become disillusioned and disappointed. Many even become depressed and start to retire from life. I've seen too many people spiral downward into poor habits largely driven by a lack of perspective, identity, values, purpose, and energy. It's sad, especially since there is a better way.

Jesus shows us a better way.

The good news is that with a little shift in perspective and some planning, there is a simple fix for this problem. When most people think about planning for retirement, all they consider is how they can accumulate more assets.

People going into retirement with plenty of assets are just as likely to be disillusioned and frustrated with retirement as those without enough assets to retire. My belief is that there are fewer people who lack the assets to retire than most people think. Our culture demands that we accumulate more in order to be successful in life and in retirement. However, research suggests that no matter the level of assets people have saved, culture leads them to believe that they still need an additional twenty-five percent to have "enough".

I happened to have the good fortune of watching other people flounder in retirement (good for me to notice, not for them to experience). I was able to question why, research the issues, explore potential answers, and to be blessed with wise counsel from mentors. I discovered the best advice was to explore what the Bible has to say about retirement, identity, values, purpose, lifestyle, money, possessions, work, and rest. In order to build our retirement on a solid foundation, we have to allow Jesus to show us a better way.

Through this observational process, my spouse, Bonnie, and I have been blessed to plan for retirement financially, as well as in other ways. In doing so, we decided that the worldly version of retirement was not for us. We also came to believe that the worldly view of retirement isn't necessarily biblical. While we were blessed to retire from full-time employment and full-time compensation a lot earlier than we thought we would, the key for us was a mind shift from "retirement" to "Renewalment".

Renewalment is nothing more or less than a new phase of life. It is simply a new life transition we've made, minus the compensation. Renewalment is a new *perspective* on retirement where we intentionally renew, refocus, and reposition where we invest our time, energy, experience, relationships, passions, wisdom, and financial resources. We achieve this through an intentional yet flexible rhythm of service, rest, vocation, and structure. (Note: I'm obviously not the first one to write about the need to view retirement differently. Mitch Anthony talks about "The New Retirementality," Ted Kaufman and Bruce Hiland note the need to pay attention to more than money and Ken Blanchard has a book "Refire! Don't Retire!" along with others. They are all great reads and have excellent retirement insights, yet not from this Renewalment perspective.)

We're busy on purpose, with purpose, yet we're not in a hurry. We can be present and available while planting seeds for God's kingdom. We can serve others through our unique rhythm and gifts. We have retired from full-time employment, yet we have not retired from life. We're blessed to live a Christ-like lifestyle of purpose, provision, contentment, and enjoyment while thriving in Christ.

It's important to note that biblically speaking, we are not called to retirement. However, we are called to be fruitful. We can remain fruitful throughout our entire life, including our retirement years.

Continuous Renewalment is an ongoing process of renewing, refocusing, and repositioning how we steward what God has entrusted to us, such as time, talents, relationships, skills, and financial treasures. We serve God by serving others and multiplying what we've been entrusted with for God's Kingdom.

We believe Renewalment can and should be the most meaningful phase of our life. It is disheartening to see numerous individuals and couples struggle in retirement. They live stuck in the life they have because they are not sure where to go, nor do they know how to move beyond their current reality. The good news is, there is a better way! There is a simple pathway to understanding *your* version (there is no one-size-fits-all) of how to thrive in Renewalment, and to ensure it is all built on a rock-solid biblical foundation.

I am passionate about wanting to help others thrive in *Renewalment.* Many people have encouraged me to write this book as a method for helping others thrive in Renewalment.

The problem is, I've never seen myself as someone who would write a book. I'm a very reluctant author, and I much prefer other methods of communication. I've procrastinated a considerable amount in the writing of this book. However, I came to the conclusion that I needed to use the discipline and structure of writing a book to organize this information for helping others and communicating the path forward. I also believe this book will facilitate other methods of communicating the material, therefore continuing to help people thrive. If it ends up helping just one person, I'm satisfied.

My experience with thriving in this new phase of life called "Renewalment" centers around prayerfully and intentionally working through a few important considerations. First, you must identify your heart and perspective when approaching the new opportunities in front of you. Additionally, you need to determine your identity, values, income ("Renewalment paycheck"), purpose, and life priorities. You will find the rhythm that's right for you through intentional dynamic planning.

I believe the key planning steps are…

1. Finding clarity of your heart-felt beliefs.
2. Finding clarity of your identity and who you are.
3. Finding clarity of your purpose, including making a difference that matters in this season.
4. Finding clarity of your core values.
5. Finding clarity of your personal wellbeing approach.
6. Finding clarity of your most valued priorities, "enough of a paycheck," *and* a simple and flexible structure to

intentionally and consistently, not perfectly, thrive in
Renewalment.

7. Living a joy-filled life of provision, contentment, generosity, and enjoyment.

... all based on a rock-solid foundation of Biblical
principles and living a Christ-like lifestyle.

I've also learned that we will all mess up along the way and fall
back into poor habits. We must be able to develop a process to
catch ourselves and work through issues such as boredom or fears
that may arise. These interruptions will take us off course and dis-
tract us from life's priorities. Working through the above seven
steps will give you the foundation you'll need to catch yourself
and pull out of these rabbit holes you may find yourself in.

Most importantly, what we do must be built on a rock-solid
foundation of biblical truth, wisdom, and principles. We are all
designed with a God-sized hole in our heart. In order to thrive,
this hole must be filled with God.

Bonnie and I have been in Renewalment for close to four years
as of this writing. We have gone through all the normal ups and
downs. Yet the lows have been minimal, and the highs are pure
enjoyment. Since we have a biblical foundation for our plan, it's
easy to get back on track knowing the foundational principles
are transcending, always true, never changing, and for our benefit.

Most people don't take the time to intentionally work through
the seven steps outlined above, or even know they exist.
Therefore, if they do any planning, it's usually only around the

accumulation of assets. It's important to set aside time prior to Renewalment or early in Renewalment to work through the steps as a couple (spousal unity is critical). For some, this takes a month or so. For others, it might take up to a year. Be intentional about revisiting the steps a few times a year. Then you'll be able to identify and learn from what is and isn't working and adjust accordingly.

I have seen some individuals and couples effectively work through the planning journey on their own, yet for most it's important to find a coach to help them intentionally work through the process, ask the necessary questions, and to hold them accountable for moving forward one step at a time.

Foundational Beliefs this Book is Based On

I believe all we need to know about money is in the Bible. There are more than 2,300 verses in the Bible that relate to money and possessions. This is more than any other topic! God knew we would struggle with money and its related topics and has provided us with timeless, transcending, always true, and never changing guidance and principles.

The Bible has guidance and wisdom for all financial decisions. The same overarching principles apply to all of us, yet we must implement them based on our specific and unique circumstances. These principles include routines for living out this financial wisdom, including a rock-solid foundation of 5 wise biblical financial principles (as outlined in Chapter 2).

The Bible also includes guidance and principles on topics like work, a life of leisure, laziness, service, and lifestyle. These principles help lay the foundation for understanding what Renewalment looks like from a biblical perspective.

From my perspective, Americans have been misled and sold a bill-of-goods regarding what retirement should look like. The cultural worldview paints a picture of retirement as a self-centered life of leisure – the "good life." Many retirees have become disillusioned by this picture because they cannot afford it. If they can afford it, "the good life" can be a dangerous downhill slope leading to spiritual, emotional, and physical death traps.

In reality, Renewalment is merely a new phase of life. It is a renewed way to serve God by serving others – being busy on purpose, with purpose, yet not in a hurry. This mind shift is critical in order to move away from the cultural view of retirement to a God-honoring experience with Renewalment. It includes finding your rhythm of service and giving back. Renewalment should also be an opportunity to focus on rest, vocation, and developing a structure that aligns with your gifts, personality, and dreams.

As mentioned, my wife, Bonnie, and I have replaced "retirement" with "Renewalment" in order to give this phase of our lives a new perspective. For us, Renewalment is where we intentionally renew, refocus, and reposition where we invest our time, energy, experience, relationships, passions, wisdom, and financial resources. This is done in an intentional, flexible rhythm of service, rest, vocation, and structure as we serve others through our unique rhythms and gifts.

We are intentional about being busy on purpose, with purpose. Yet, we are not in a hurry.

Thriving in this new phase of life centers around prayerfully and intentionally working through a variety of opportunities that will arise, your life priorities, and finding the rhythm that's right for you through intentional dynamic planning.

This book will walk you through each of these issues and opportunities, as well as help you answer the questions that can come with them. I will present you with research on the topic, what the Bible has to say, biblical principles, my experiences and observations, and a call-to-action challenge.

> *"For even the Son of Man did not come to be served, but to serve, and to give His life as a ransom for many."* (Mark 10:45 NIV)

We will also explore additional questions you might have, such as:

- When should I start to plan and prepare for retirement?
- How can this new phase of life be the best phase ever?
- What does it mean to live a God-pleasing life in retirement? Do I want to?
- What does a Christian lifestyle look like?
- Is my financial plan built on a rock-solid foundation?
- Who will I be in retirement? Will I lose my identity?
- Will I be relevant?
- Do biblical principles still apply today, and are they relevant?

Renewalment is merely a new phase of life. It is essential to prepare, plan, and discern from a heart perspective as you transition into this new phase. Determining your perspective based on identity, purpose, core values, and income is critical. Approaching Renewalment with an eternal viewpoint and dynamic planning will ensure that it is the most rewarding phase of life! — Bruce Fear

"When it comes to planning, many Christians act like atheists. They realize Jesus saved them, but they don't really trust him. They think they can plan their life any way they want to. But the reality is that God created everyone and made each person for a unique purpose. He has a specific destiny for everyone." — Rick Warren[1]

"Biblical principles are timeless, authoritative, always true, and never change." — Ron Blue

Building on Ron's quote... I believe biblical principles are timeless, authentic, always true, never change and apply the same for all and will be uniquely and thoughtfully applied in prayer and discernment to your life situation as you learn and adjust over time. One size does not fit all.

"Counsel and sound judgment are mine; I have insight, I have power...[B]y me princes govern, and nobles—all who rule on earth...With me are riches and honor, enduring wealth and prosperity. My

*fruit is better than fine gold; what I yield surpasses
choice silver."* (Proverbs 8:14, 16, 18–19 NIV)

A few of the products of biblical wisdom: All things that create
success—the right plan (counsel), the strategic resourcefulness
to carry it out (sound judgment), and the boldness to execute
(power) – belong to wisdom. Any accomplishment that is not
mere luck is grounded in the attributes of wisdom.

*"Fear of the Lord leads to life, bringing security and
protection from harm."* (Proverbs 19:23 NLT)

Are you open to exploring a path to help you thrive in
Renewalment, including a God-pleasing life of provision, contentment, and enjoyment?

If your answer is yes, read on.

Chapter 1

DISILLUSIONMENT OF RETIREMENT

IN MY EXPERIENCE, many retirees become totally disillusioned with the picture of retirement American society has developed and sold. There's a lie that suggests the goal of retirement is a self-centered life of leisure, or a "retired from life" phase.

Numerous Americans are disillusioned with this cultural worldview of retirement. Their disappointment often stems from not being able to afford this worldly version of retirement. Those who *can* afford it become disillusioned with the emptiness and lack of enjoyment they experience in a self-centered, self-absorbed lifestyle.

I'd suggest the emptiness experienced by many in retirement is due to the fact we are not designed to retire; we are designed to work and to serve, to add value and find fulfillment; to mentor and encourage. There are times when transitioning to a new phase of life, regardless of age, may be very appropriate. We may enter a phase of life where we find our own unique rhythm of service, rest, vocation, and structure. However, a transition to a self-centered life of leisure is not part of the design. Note: Leisure is good, just not as a lifestyle – more on that later.

We are not biblically called to enter retirement, but we are called to live a life worthy of the Lord, please Him in every way, bear fruit in very good work, and grow in the knowledge of God (Colossians 1:10).

Why People Retire

If there is a general disillusionment with retirement, then why do people retire? First of all, they don't know there's a better approach. They've bought into the cultural lie that tells us the goal is a life of leisure and accumulating more. This is the clear message being promoted and sold by the retirement and financial service communities.

According to a 2016 Willis Towers Watson[1] survey, people retire for the following reasons.

- Personal (64%) – life of leisure, health issues, service
- Employer (56%) – pension eligibility, lay-offs
- Anchors (24%) – eligible for social security or Medicare, triggers
- Workplace (23%) – freedom from onerous work, lack enthusiasm, not valued
- Family (22%) – time with family, take care of family
- Job Capacity (14%) – unable to physically do the job

It appears the majority of Americans retire largely based on the "retirement lie." The lie manifests in a variety of incorrect beliefs. "You've lost your worth as a worker." "You've earned a self-centered life of leisure." "It's the fun life you deserve!" "Someone owes it to you once you reach some arbitrary age."

Frankly, the truth is you haven't "earned" anything and you're not "owed" anything.

According to a study[2], people choose to retire "early" for five key reasons:

- Layoffs
- Health
- Caring for family
- Freedom to pursue interests
- Dissatisfaction with career

Layoffs and health concerns may be out of a person's control, yet they don't necessarily need to lead to retirement. The other three reasons are a matter of personal choice. They may very well necessitate a life transition, but not an unplanned "retirement."

And what is "early" retirement? Early compared to what?

Compared to some arbitrary age of sixty-five that's centered around when most people become eligible for Social Security Benefits? Compared to a retirement age set when the average life expectancy was only fifty-eight to sixty-five years of age? Why are we putting our hopes of retiring into a system designed primarily as a safety net with old-age benefits for workers, benefits

3

for victims of industrial accidents, unemployment insurance, aid for dependent mothers and children, or the blind and physically handicapped?

There is nothing magical about the age of sixty-five. Making a life transition at this age might work for the masses, but it is very arbitrary for the individual. Yet this age seems to be the magic number that drives Americans to retire. It's set as an arbitrary anchor for when people should do something, according to a government program. Perhaps you should consider your "retirement date" based on your life priorities, not an arbitrary age or government program.

Are you merely a follower? Or are you an individual with the ability to make decisions based on your own life priorities instead of someone else's priorities or expectations for you?

Why People Don't Retire

Many people choose not to retire at age sixty-five. Others make the decision not to retire at all.

A recent Wells Fargo study found that thirty-four percent of respondents believe they won't retire until they're at least eighty years old. An even larger number of people (thirty-seven percent) said they will never retire and believe they will continue to work until they are either too sick or they die.

Is your idea of "the good life" working just to work because you don't know what else you'd do, or working until you fall over dead? Is that your idea of a fulfilling retirement? It doesn't sound like a life of contentment or enjoyment to me.

A lack of financial planning can be one perceived reason people choose not to retire. Many people have convinced themselves of the lie that they can't afford to retire, yet they haven't actually done the planning to really know for sure. People often use it as an excuse for a perceived "deeper" reason, which is often simply to accumulate more. Fear of financial loss is significant. People may have concerns about losing the security of fringe benefits and without a plan for the future, may choose to avoid retirement.

It has also become evident that many non-financial factors have a significant impact on choosing not to retire. These factors can contribute to negative psychological effects in retirement.

Psychological effects of disengagement between a work life and the transition to retirement[3]:

- Partial identity disruption
- Decision paralysis
- Diminished self-trust
- Experience of a post retirement void
- The search for meaningful engagement in society
- Development of a retirement life structure
- The confluence of aging and retirement
- Experiencing anxiety about death
- The critical nurturing of social relationships
- Self-actualization

People often fear potential emotional and personal losses in retirement. When people enter a new phase of life, they often wonder if they will lose their identity and purpose. Will they be able to maintain friendships, community, energy, self- esteem, and their role in their home life? *Making retirement decisions out of fear, regardless of what that fear is, does not lead to thriving in retirement.* My experience is that people use a lot of fear-based excuses not to retire, or they retire to an unplanned life of misery. The real issues stem from a lack of thoughtful planning to address their fears.

Not having a retirement plan may turn out all right for the few who die an unexpected death, but it's not a valid plan for everyone else.

Retirement, or any phase-of-life transition, requires intentional thought with biblical guidance on the path designed for you to take. It's important to have clarity and resolution when it comes to your heart/perspective opportunities, your identity/ purpose opportunities, your core values, your vocation, your income opportunities, and your life priorities. Being purposefully, meaningfully, and productively engaged in life is crucial for a well-adjusted retirement.

Why People are Disillusioned

People are disillusioned about retirement because they are buying into a false set of expectations and they don't prepare and plan for their transition into this phase of life. If they've done any planning, it's most likely focused only on the accumulation of assets. Having the discipline to save for retirement is important, yet the critical planning and preparation needs to be more focused on your heart perspective, your identity and purpose, your core values, your life priorities, your vocation, and then your income path.

We are created to serve God through serving others, not ourselves. A self-centered focus while living a life of leisure leaves a big hole in both your heart and soul. This is the key reason for most of the disillusionment people have with retirement. I believe we have a God-sized hole in our heart, and true contentment happens only when we walk daily with Jesus.

In his book *My Plan for Living to 156: Imaginatively extend your lifetime to transform how you live in the present*[4], Dan Sullivan suggests we should eliminate the idea of retirement from our thought process.

> We retire factory equipment, we retire battleships, and we retire resources. The term "retirement" means to be taken out of use. By its very nature, retirement means that a decision has been made that you're no longer useful.

> When sixty-five was established as the retirement age in the United States, the average lifespan in the country was fifty-eight. The government saw this as a way of taking in money that they'd never have to pay out. Retirement was created for political reasons and for reasons related to repetitive work that tires people out.

> Your age shouldn't dictate how useful you are, and your usefulness should go beyond "keeping up."

Most people talk themselves into slowing down and wrapping things up, but you don't have to be one of those people. Eliminate any kind of thinking and talking that would persuade you that at a certain point in your life, you're supposed to "go downhill."

Never retiring means constantly recreating yourself. And if you want to constantly recreate yourself, you have to constantly create new projects. There's no reason to concentrate on bringing all your work to completion, except to take it to a higher level.

Always be starting new projects, investments, and relationships. Don't entertain ideas like having a "bucket list" or leaving a legacy, because those are thoughts that include you no longer having a future.

Personal Story

I told myself, most of my life, that I would never retire. I said things like, "I love to work," and "I love my job and the people I work with!" All of these statements were true. But in reality, my biggest issue was fear. Fear of failure was only part of it. I also wrestled with worry over not having enough income or not being able to solve problems by throwing money at them. Finally, I had concerns over not being (looking) generous or appearing lazy. The material that follows in this little book helped me work through my fears and plan for the future, all while living for today and eventually thriving in Renewalment. I believe that you also can thrive with the right approach within your unique personality and circumstances. It can all be done when choosing to stand on a rock-solid foundation of biblical principles.

Path Forward

People retire for any number of reasons. Financial issues impact our retirement decisions. However, spiritual and emotional issues are just as important and are frequently left out of the decision-making process, which is a mistake. Key reasons people choose not to retire are greed, fear, lack of knowledge, lack of a plan, and lack of seeing a better way. Not having a retirement plan may turn out all right for the few who die a quick, unexpected death, but it's not a valid plan for everyone else.

Being intentional, seeking and listening to God's guidance, and discerning His will for this phase of your life is critical to thriving in Renewalment. It requires building on a rock-solid foundation of biblical principles along with dynamic planning and preparing from a heart perspective, clarity of identity and purpose, identifying core values, life priorities, vocation clarity, and clarity of your monthly "retirement paycheck."

The goal is to help you intentionally seek out the data and information you need in order to understand your options, and to then seek counsel and biblical wisdom to discern your path. Ask, "God, what would you have me do?"

There is a path forward for everyone. The Bible has the answers to a path of provision, contentment, and enjoyment! You can

- and should - thrive in your life transitions. This includes Renewalment!

As you work your way through this book, you'll develop your unique path forward. Together, we'll take the time to understand what the Bible says about retirement and related topics, and to reframe your perspective on retirement. You'll learn how to discern your heart perspective, identity and sense of purpose, core values, and life priorities along with vocation options in Renewalment. We will help you gain perspective and confidence in your provision income plan, as well as gain clarity of your desired rhythm structure. We'll help you walk through each step and determine your path forward.

***

Take a few minutes to write down your responses to the following question. It's important to name your fears and write them down in order to address them.

- What are my fears, concerns, and disillusionments about retirement?

Please note that you'll get more out of this book when you take the time to respond to the questions and actually write down the answers that are uniquely yours.

Chapter 2

BIBLICAL PRINCIPLES

AMERICANS HAVE BEEN sold a bill of goods. They've been led to think that retirement is about a self-centered life of leisure versus merely a new phase of life. This was not the intention of our Creator! We were created to serve God through serving others, not ourselves. We can retire from full-time work for pay, but we cannot retire from a life of serving God. A self-centered focus through a life of leisure leaves a big hole in your heart and soul. This is the key reason for most of the disillusionment people have with retirement. We are designed with a God-sized hole in our heart. True contentment happens only when we walk daily with Jesus – including during Renewalment.

We are not called to retire from life. You were created to "bear fruit" (Genesis 1:22). God is glorified when you "bear much fruit" (John 15:8), and God has great plans for you even in retirement.

The Lord should be first in our lives and to be the center of our affections. He urges us to store up treasures in heaven by caring for the lost and hurting people around us – not just prior to retirement, but throughout every phase of our lives. Gratitude and serving others are two keys to thriving in retirement. If you're ever feeling down, look at all you have to be grateful for and then go help someone else. The quickest path to joy is through gratitude and generosity.

On whom is your attention focused?

Do you wonder what a Christian lifestyle should look like?
Do you desire to live a life pleasing to God?
Do you desire to live a life based on biblical principles?
Do you desire to live your retirement years in a God-pleasing manner based on biblical principles?
Do you want to ask and discern the question, "God, do you have a purpose for my life in Renewalment?"

As Rick Warren, senior pastor of Saddleback Church, points out, *"When it comes to planning, many Christians act like atheists. They realize Jesus saved them, but they don't really trust him. They think they can plan their life any way they want to. But the reality is that God created everyone and made each person for a unique purpose. He has a specific destiny for everyone."*[1]

So where do we look for guidance? Since biblical principles are timeless, authoritative, always true, and never change, it seems like it might be wise to build your Renewalment plan on the rock-solid foundation of biblical principles. Do you agree?

Keep in mind, biblical principles aren't always a "one-size-fits-all" situation. The same biblical principles apply to all of us, but they need to be applied to our unique circumstances. We should not attempt to alter biblical truth, yet apply it to our individual situation.

Let's take a look at what the Bible has to say about work, a life of leisure/laziness, the Christian lifestyle, vocation, wise financial principles, and the biblical view of retirement.

Biblical View of Work

The Bible offers an abundance of wisdom on the topic of work. These five biblical ideas on work from Billy Graham[2] may help you view work in a new light.

1. Work is a gift from God. (Genesis 2:15)

    Since the beginning, work has been part of God's plan for humanity. He created it. That means you can view the act of working as a gift, even if you don't love your job.

2. Those who are able to work should do so.

    Both the Old and New Testaments of the Bible speak highly of work and condemn laziness.

3. Work like God is your boss. (Colossians 3:23-24)

4. Take time to rest. (Exodus 20:8-10)

    Our work was never meant to become the center of our lives.

5. Put God first when you plan for old age.

The Bible doesn't specifically address the current-day concept of retirement, which is a relatively new idea. We do know that many of the Bible's best-known servants of God never stopped working for the Lord, even when they were quite old.

God designed work for each of us. Work is good! God designed each of us with our unique DNA. Each of us were made on purpose for a purpose, and each of us have been entrusted with spiritual gifts. God designed work or vocation for one's entire life lived in response to His calling. This calling is not only for our time prior to retirement, it's meant for our entire life. Yes, what it looks like and is implemented will most likely change through our various life transitions and life phases we experience. However, we are called to a life of service and to live a life of purpose, on purpose.

> *"When we use our abilities to help each other, God is glorified. The Bible says, 'God has given each of you a gift from his great variety of spiritual gifts. Use them well to serve one another.'*[3] *(1 Peter 4:10 NLT).* — *Rick Warren*

> *"As you do your work with integrity and justice, God is glorified. The God who is exalted above the heavens can also be lifted up in your daily work."* — Mark Roberts

Biblical View of a Life of Leisure and Laziness

Its clear God designed us for work, and the Bible gives numerous warnings against laziness.

- *"Those who work their land will have abundant food, but those who chase fantasies have no sense."* (Proverbs 12:11 NIV)
- *"Diligent hands will rule, but laziness ends in forced labor."* (Proverbs 12:24 NIV)
- *"A sluggard's appetite is never filled, but the desires of the diligent are fully satisfied."* (Proverbs 13:4 NIV)
- *"Go to the ant, you sluggard; consider its ways and be wise! It has no commander, no overseer or ruler, yet it stores its provisions in summer and gathers its food at harvest."* (Proverbs 6:6-8 NIV)
- *"The craving of a sluggard will be the death of him, because his hands refuse to work."* (Proverbs 21:25 NIV)

The Bible makes two clear prohibitions:

- Idleness... *"Slothfulness casts into a deep sleep, and an idle person will suffer hunger."* (Proverbs 19:15 ESV)
- Self-Focused Pleasure... *"Or do you not know that your body is a temple of the Holy Spirit within you, whom you have from God? You are not your own, for you were bought with a price. So glorify God in your body."* (1 Corinthians 6:19-20 ESV)

Our work, before and after retirement, should be centered on service to others, not solely on ourselves. We don't earn the right to become self-centered and inward focused simply by working at a job until age sixty-five. These are prime years for serving others in love and giving back.

> *Do nothing out of selfish ambition or vain conceit. Rather, in humility value others above yourselves, not looking to your own interests but each of you to the interests of the others.* (Philippians 2:3-4 NIV)

God owns it all. We are to be stewards of what He has blessed us with and to multiply through God's economics. The use of our resources - the resources God has entrusted to our care - should be directed by God before and after retirement, as well as throughout Renewalment.

> *Command those who are rich in this present world not to be arrogant nor to put their hope in wealth, which is so uncertain, but to put their hope in God, who richly provides us with everything for our enjoyment. Command them to do good, to be rich in good deeds, and to be generous and willing to share. In this way they will lay up treasure for themselves as a firm foundation for the coming age, so that they may take hold of the life that is truly life.* — (1 Timothy 6:17-19 NIV)

Work is good; laziness is not. Yet we can't let a longing for success become the driving force in our lives. If we do, we will lose sight of the abundant life Jesus offers and instead become engrossed in the never-ending, unattainable images of perfection.

We are created for a purpose, on purpose, to make a difference no one else can. God made you uniquely for a unique role only you can fill.

Biblical View of the Christian Lifestyle

The Christian call is to live like Christ and to become more like Jesus. It's impossible for us to be exactly like Jesus, yet we can and are expected to strive to become more like Jesus on a daily basis. As we take steps forward, we will undoubtedly take steps backward – it's our sinful nature. Yet when we do, we continue to be intentional about moving forward, becoming more like Jesus. No matter what happens, we can be confident that we were created on purpose, for a purpose.

While the Bible doesn't specifically identify the "right" Christian lifestyle, 1 Timothy provides clear biblical principles for the lifestyle we are to live; a life of provision, contentment, and enjoyment.

Provision: *Anyone who does not provide for their relatives, and especially for their own household, has denied the faith and is worse than an unbeliever.* (1 Timothy 5:8 NIV)

Contentment: *But godliness with contentment is great gain. For we brought nothing into the world, and we can take nothing out of it. But if we have food and clothing, we will be content with that.* (1 Timothy 6:6-8 NIV)

> Enjoyment: *Command those who are rich in this present world not to be arrogant nor to put their hope in wealth, which is so uncertain, but to put their hope in God, who richly provides us with everything for our enjoyment.* (1 Timothy 6:17 NIV)

We are called to provide for our family and others in order to meet our spiritual, emotional, relational, physical, and financial needs. We are to balance this with a heartfelt contentment and peace with what God has chosen to entrust us with – spiritual gifts and treasures – while seeking to intentionally multiply these gifts and treasures. We are called to do this based on God's economy, not the cultural view of "more for me". And we're expected to find joy in what we do, who we do it with, and whom we do it for.

We must avoid the comparison trap – it's a cancer to the soul and will eat away at our spiritual, emotional, relational, physical, and financial health. Comparison will rob you of a life of contentment and enjoyment.

The article, "What Should a Christ-Centered Life Look Like?"[4] suggests the following:

A Christ-centered life is…

- Focused upon a commitment to Jesus, including getting to know Him, enjoying Him, and bringing Him glory. (Isaiah 43:7; 2 Corinthians 3:18; John 17: 1-5, 22).
- Focused on the primary goal of glorifying God.

- The pursuit of God as its highest-calling…to become more like Jesus.
- Making the glory of Christ the orienting compass that gives direction to all other goals.
- Making decisions based on the question "Would this please God?"
- Having hope in eternity, and hope in the here and now.

A Christ-centered life is not…

- Focused on religion/law.
- Self-centered.
- Being "perfect." We will stumble.

When you center your life on God, you start to become more like Him. A life fully surrendered to God will naturally produce godly qualities. When a Christ-centered person stumbles, they quickly confess the sin and restore fellowship with Him. (Note: you cannot do this without an intentional structure that fits you. More on the importance of structure later).

The human heart was designed for worship, and if it does not worship God, it will worship something else. That which we center our lives on can become our god. Will it be the tri-une-God or will it be something else? The Bible makes it clear you cannot worship both God and money (or any other small, false god you're most focused on).

A Christ-like lifestyle can only be found when we walk daily with Jesus, intentionally and consistently.

Each one should test their own actions. Then they can take pride in themselves alone, without comparing themselves to someone else. (Galatians 6:4 NIV)

Biblical View of Vocation (Calling)

Webster defines vocation as "a strong desire to spend your life doing a certain kind of work (such as religious work); the work a person does or should be doing; a summons or strong inclination to a particular state or course of action."

Okay, not really a lot of help. Perhaps some insights from Martin Luther[5] will be helpful.

> "For Martin Luther, vocation is nothing less than the locus of the Christian life. God works in and through vocation, but he does so by calling human beings to work in their vocations. In Jesus Christ, who bore our sins and gives us new life in His resurrection, God saves us for eternal life. But in the meantime He places us in our temporal life where we grow in faith and holiness. In our various callings — as spouse, parent, church member, citizen, and worker — we are to live out our faith.
>
> So, what does it mean to live out our faith in our callings? The Bible is clear: faith bears fruit in love (Gal. 5:6; 1 Tim. 1:5). Here we come to justification by faith and its relationship to good works, and we also encounter the ethical

implications of vocation. According to Luther's doctrine of vocation, the purpose of every vocation is to love and serve our neighbors.

Loving and Serving Our Neighbors

God does not need our good works, Luther said, but our neighbor does (Wingren, *Luther on Vocation*, 10). Our relationship with God is based completely on His work for us in the life, death, and resurrection of Christ. Justification by faith completely excludes any kind of dependence on our good works for our salvation. We come before God clothed not in our own works or merits, but solely in the works and merits of Christ, which are imputed to us. But having been justified by faith, we are sent by God back into the world, into our vocations, to love and serve our neighbors."

Vocation will likely change during various life transitions, including Renewalment. Yet, living the vocation you're called to does not stop just because you retire from a career. Your vocation might change (renew or refocus) when you retire from your job, but your purpose to serve God by serving others never stops or retires. Retirement does not give us permission to accept the cultural worldview of retiring to a self-centered life of leisure. Yes, we should incorporate rest, travel, and vacations into this new phase of life. However, those should not be the primary focus. Instead, you can find a blend of rhythm, service, rest, vocation, and structure that best fits the unique gifts God has given you.

Another perspective on vocation comes from Ron Blue, founder of the Ronald Blue Company, Kingdom Advisors, and the Ron Blue Institute for Financial Planning[6]. Blue provides a four-point summary of vocation:

1. Everyone is designed uniquely by God.

> *"For you created my inmost being; you knit me together in my mother's womb. I praise you because I am fearfully and wonderfully made; your works are wonderful, I know that full well."* (Psalm 139:13-14 NIV)

2. Everyone has been given gifts for a purpose.

> *"We have different gifts, according to the grace given to each of us. If your gift is prophesying, then prophesy in accordance with your faith; if it is serving, then serve; if it is teaching, then teach; if it is to encourage, then give encouragement; if it is giving, then give generously; if it is to lead, do it diligently; if it is to show mercy, do it cheerfully."* (Romans 12:6-8 NIV)

3. Everyone should develop his or her gifts for excellence.

> *"Do you see someone skilled in their work? They will serve before kings; they will not serve before officials of low rank."* (Proverbs 22:29 NIV)

4. Work is a stage by which you can glorify God.

"In the same way, let your light shine before others, that they may see your good deeds and glorify your Father in heaven." (Matthew 5:16 NIV)

"Some wake up to an alarm. Some wake up to a calling." – Unknown

Vocation is more than a job; it's a calling. It helps give you purpose and a path for making a difference in the world beyond yourself. A job tends to focus on paying the bills, but a vocation helps make a difference by serving God through serving others. A job and a vocation can be the same, overlap, or be totally separate. *What matters is that they're done for the glory of God.*

The combination of job and vocation will most likely change over time, representing different seasons as we go through life transitions. Frequently ask yourself the question, "What is the 'best' blend of vocation, work, service, and rest for me?" This dynamic question needs to be asked periodically since the answer will change as your life changes. Don't focus on finding the exact "right" answer. Instead, discern the best one for now, then act, learn, and adjust. Your intent and *whom* you're doing it for (to whose glory), is more important than exactly *what* you do.

Instead of asking yourself, "What is my vocation," the more important question is, "How will I determine the best opportunity currently presented to me?" Discover the answer God has for you in this moment through prayer, scripture, obedience, reflection, and counsel of fellow believers.

The Bible makes it clear that we should practice our vocation until the day we die. The call for service to God and others never stops. While your vocation may change several times through various seasons of life, it does not stop at some specific age set by a cultural worldview, with a self-centered, inward focused lifestyle. We may not know what our vocation will be over the next several decades, but we can discern and trust God to lead us one step at a time. This process is a journey of faith in which God provides evolving options, depending upon our choices and the choices of others.

Continually seek God's will, listening with patience and taking courageous action. Simply listen, trust, and obey God.

Biblical View of Wise Financial Principles

> "For where your treasure is, there your heart will be also." (Matthew 6:21 & Luke 12:34)

The Bible has more than 2,300 verses on money-related topics. It is the focus of more than half of Jesus' parables. It appears as if "someone" knew we would struggle with issues related to money and possessions! Yet the answers are in plain sight. All you need to know about money can be found in the Bible. The Bible provides information, guidance, principles, and wisdom for all financial decisions.

The question is whether or not you will be obedient to God's guidance.

Over the course of your lifetime, you will face numerous financial issues that accompany life transitions. These issues may include taxes, wealth management and transfer, inheritance, saving and giving, and debt. Life transitions are important topics to discuss. However, the secret to financial success, no matter what stage of life you're in, is found in your daily money routines. More complex strategies can be helpful on the margins, but the real opportunity comes from wisdom and clarity in getting the "small" stuff right.

So how do you get the "small" stuff right? I believe the Bible outlines 5 Wise Financial Principles[7] for day-to-day financial living. These key biblical principles are universal to everyone, yet they need to be uniquely applied based on individual circumstances through your unique Spending Plan (more on Spending Plans later). The five wise principles include:

1. **Spend Less Than You Earn (Renewalment Income)**

   o Money is meant to be a tool, not our master. We cannot serve both money and God. The real question may be, "Who am I serving?"
   o *"Lazy hands make for poverty, but diligent hands bring wealth."* (Proverbs 10:4 NIV)

2. **Be Wise with Debt**

   o Acquiring debt is not a sin, yet it is dangerous because debt can easily become your master. Debt also reduces and eliminates your choices and options. You do not want to be a "slave" to debt.

o *"The rich rule over the poor, and the borrower is slave to the lender."* (Proverbs 22:7 NIV)

o *"The wicked borrow and do not repay, but the righteous give generously."* (Psalm 37:21 NIV)

3. Build Margin and Protect Yourself Against Setbacks

o Building financial margin is the key to meeting long-term goals and finding financial freedom. You also need a plan to protect against the derailers of life.

o *"Go to the ant, you sluggard; consider its ways and be wise! It has no commander, no overseer or ruler, yet it stores its provisions in summer and gathers its food at harvest."* (Proverbs 6:6-8 NIV)

o *"Suppose one of you wants to build a tower. Won't you first sit down and estimate the cost to see if you have enough money to complete it?"* (Luke 14:28 NIV)

o *"A prudent person foresees danger and takes precautions. The simpleton goes blindly on and suffers the consequences."* (Proverbs 22:3 NLT)

4. Have Long-Term Goals

o Long-term goals give you direction and are the key to identifying short-term priorities, routines, habits, and discipline.

o *"For we are God's handiwork, created in Christ Jesus to do good works, which God prepared in advance for us to do."* (Ephesians 2:10 NIV) o *"I press on toward the goal to win the prize for which God has called me heavenward in Christ Jesus."* (Philippians 3:14 NIV)

5. Live Generously – Give Back

o You can't afford not to give. Tithing is a test of your trust. God doesn't need your money. Giving is an opportunity for you to put your faith into practice.
o The shortest path to joy is through gratitude and generosity.
o *"And here is my judgment about what is best for you in this matter. Last year you were the first not only to give but also to have the desire to do so. Now finish the work, so that your eager willingness to do it may be matched by your completion of it, according to your means."* (2 Corinthians 8:10-11 NIV)

Considering these five wise financial principles, which do you feel the best about? Which do you have the least confidence in?

NOTE: The only way to achieve your long-term financial goals is through the building of financial margin. This requires the incorporation of the five biblical financial principles into your daily routines, both as an individual and as a family. Family unity around the incorporation of these principles is critical to your success. **The key to building financial margin is to spend less than you earn, and to do it over a long period of time.** To do this you will need the flexible structure of a unique Spending Plan. Most of us will not have the need for the more advanced strategies, yet we will all benefit from the wisdom of the day-to-day principles for financial freedom. (If you're in need of or have the opportunity for more advanced financial strategies, seek out a professional Christian financial advisor known as a Certified Kingdom Advisor (CKA)).

The surest way to create wealth is to spend less than you earn and to save over a long period of time. Consistently spending less than you earn (before and during retirement), will require the development of new routines (habits), a spending plan, and a sense of contentment with what you have today. Just having more is not the answer. *If you're not content with what God has entrusted you with today, you will not be content with twice as much.*

> *"Whoever loves money never has enough; whoever loves wealth is never satisfied with their income. This too is meaningless."* (Ecclesiastes 5:10 NIV)

When you think of investing money, you might only think of investing your dollars into a variety of securities, such as the stock market or bond market. Yet there are numerous things outside of securities where we invest our dollars. The reality is there are a number of places we should invest our dollars before we even consider investing in securities. The Investment Pyramid[8] shown below provides a visual representation of the order in which you should invest your dollars to create a strong financial foundation. It shows how to develop financial margin in order to build toward financial freedom. It's not entirely linear, and some of the steps may overlap. Yet, it reveals the necessary hierarchy for developing financial freedom on a rock-solid foundation of biblical principles.

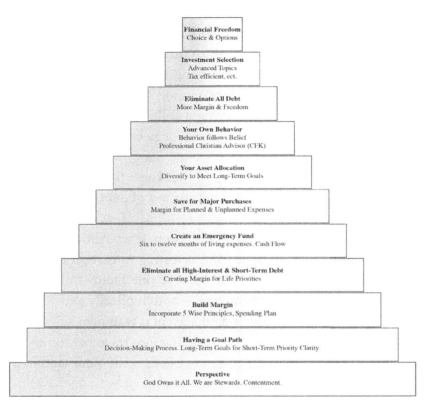

Financial Freedom
Choice & Options

Investment Selection
Advanced Topics
Tax efficient, ect.

Eliminate All Debt
More Margin & Freedom

Your Own Behavior
Behavior follows Belief
Professional Christian Advisor (CFK)

Your Asset Allocation
Diversify to Meet Long-Term Goals

Save for Major Purchases
Margin for Planned & Unplanned Expenses

Create an Emergency Fund
Six to twelve months of living expenses. Cash Flow

Eliminate all High-Interest & Short-Term Debt
Creating Margin for Life Priorities

Build Margin
Incorporate 5 Wise Principles, Spending Plan

Having a Goal Path
Decision-Making Process. Long-Term Goals for Short-Term Priority Clarity.

Perspective
God Owns it All. We are Stewards. Contentment.

(Investment Pyramid)

The first three building blocks (Perspective, Having a Goal Path, and Build Margin) focus on developing routines for successful habits on the rock-solid foundation of biblical principles. We are creatures of our habits, good and bad. The habits we develop through life from the cultural worldview tend to lead us to a plan of instability. Developing routines for successful habits on a rock-solid foundation of biblical principles and wisdom is the foundation of financial success.

Building blocks four, five and six (Eliminate all High-Interest & Short-Term Debt, Create an Emergency Fund, and Save for Major Purchases) focus on routines for creating financial margin both now and in the future. Planned and unplanned issues happen in life, and having cash flow margin to work through them is critical. Having a fully funded 401k doesn't help when your car needs a battery or new tires, or when the hot water heater needs repair. Create margin for the planned and unplanned circumstances in life. Cash flow is critical to meet immediate needs and avoid the use of debt.

Building blocks seven and eight (Your Asset Allocation and Your Own Behavior) move from investing in margin building to investing in securities. The number one factor for market investing success is diversification – both biblically and statistically. The number one investing deterrent is your own behavior – making emotional decisions and falling into the most common biases. (Overcoming your common biases is the value-add of a qualified professional financial advisor.)

> *"Invest in seven ventures, yes, in eight; you do not know what disaster may come upon the land."*
> (Ecclesiastes 11:2 NIV)

Building block nine (Eliminating all Debt) is a personal choice. There is no biblical prohibition on debt, yet there are numerous warnings about taking on debt. The reality is the borrower becomes a "slave" to the lender. Any debt needs to be repaid, both legally and morally. This limits your financial flexibility in the future. The elimination of debt provides more financial margin to make additional choices surrounding money, time, focus, and legacy.

Building block ten (Investment Selection) provides an opportunity to venture into advanced topics like tax efficiency. These topics are beneficial on the margins, and would be areas in which to seek specialized expertise. Yet true financial wealth involves saving money through the development of margin by spending less than you earn over a long period of time, and having less debt is important since it affords more choices and flexibility.

Living into building blocks one through ten are a key part of the path to financial freedom. You'll have more financial choices and options when you truly need them. You do not need to feel trapped by debt and lack of financial margin when faced with decision-making.

However, it's important to understand there is no such thing as financial security. Only God gives security. Yet by following financial biblical principles, you can experience financial freedom of choice. This is a key part in finding provision, contentment, and enjoyment.

I became a "budget person" at a young age. In hindsight, it came from a selfish perspective. My focus was on how I could budget what I spent in order to focus on myself and the things I wanted. I had little, if any, consideration about helping others or meeting long-term priorities. I hardly even had a glimpse of what my own priorities were.

While having a budget for the sake of having a budget seemed like a good idea, it also felt hollow and directionless. However, I wasn't taking the initiative to do anything about it.

While making a presentation on preparing for retirement (specifically on saving and structuring assets for retirement) one of the participants challenged me to the specifics of identifying a biblical view in relation to retirement. While I had very general, vague, and perhaps only partially correct thoughts, I wasn't confident in a response. So, I started to research what the Bible has to say about money... and WOW! There are thousands of verses about money and possessions in the Bible, and at least half of Jesus' parables relate to money or our possessions. I pored over verses and chapters of the Bible along with numerous books and articles on biblical truths about finances. I also attended various presentations to solidify my knowledge of biblical truth as it relates to retirement.

Learning what the Bible has to say about money, work, and retirement was a game changer for Bonnie and me. (It actually led to "retiring" at age fifty-nine when I originally thought I might work until seventy.)

Over time, intentionally and consistently aligning with the five wise biblical financial principles, I gained new insights on using money as a tool or a means to an end, rather than as an end in and of itself. Instead of just creating a budget, we designed a Spending Plan aligned with meeting our long-term goals as a family. The process of developing our spending plan was clarifying, and it helped strengthen spousal communication and unity around finances and other topics. A budget tends to bring the mindset of cutting back and being restrictive. A spending plan is a mindset of how you align your spending with your life priorities.

It's common sense, I suppose. But it was freeing and reassuring to clearly see that the path to building financial margin is to intentionally and consistently spend less than you earn over time rather than some magical investment such as stock, bond, cryptocurrency, or real estate.

True financial freedom came with the realization that human-made financial security is a myth. Only God can provide true security, and financial freedom is about following biblical principles and being in a position to have financial choices and options when life happens. I also came to the realization that I can't out-give God.

This all came to light through a series of conversations with Ron Blue, along with reading his books and listening to presentations. Yet the real impact came when Ron directly asked me what our giving plan was. At the time, our "plan" was to give, tithe, and do some other good stuff when it came about. His question helped me realize that we really didn't have a plan! We needed an intentional, values-focused, priorities-aligned giving plan. So we committed to developing a giving plan that, from a dollar amount, seemed to be ridiculous. It was way more than we'd ever given before, and more than I'd earned a few years prior. With faith and mostly through God's blessings, we exceeded the giving plan numbers, and our overall finances actually improved. How did that happen?

It was through God's economics, not man's.

Biblical View of Retirement

The following describes several views on what the Bible says about retirement.

What does the Bible say about retirement? Is retirement biblical? A four-point response from *Got Questions. Your Questions. Biblical Answers*[9]...

1. There is no biblical principle that states a person should retire from his work when reaching a certain age. The only reference to retirement is in Numbers – the Levite males are numbered for service in the tabernacle to age 50, then they are to retire from regular service. They are to continue to "assist their brothers." (Numbers 4; 8:24-26)

2. Even though we may retire from our vocation, we should never retire from serving the Lord; the way we serve Him may change. (Luke 2:25-38, Titus 2)

3. One's older years are not to be spent solely in the pursuit of pleasure. Paul says the widow who lives for pleasure is dead while she yet lives (1 Timothy 5:6). Contrary to biblical instruction, many people equate retirement with the "pursuit of pleasure." Not to say we can't or shouldn't enjoy golf, social functions, and other pleasurable pursuits. But they should not be the primary focus of one's life at any age.

4. 2 Corinthians 12:14 states that parents ought to save up for the children. But by far the greatest thing to "save up" is one's spiritual heritage, which can be passed on to children, grandchildren and great-grandchildren. Prayer

is perhaps the most fruitful ministry outlet for those who have retired.

The Christian never retires from Christ's service; he only changes the address of his workplace. As one reaches "retirement age" their work or vocation may change, but one's life work of serving the Lord does not.

"Even when I am old and gray, do not forsake me, my God, till I declare your power to the next generation, your might to all who are to come." (Psalm 71:18 NIV)

O.S. Hawkins on "Is Retirement Biblical"[10]? (emphasis added)

- There is certainly not a prohibition of it in the Bible. There is only one reference to what we understand as retirement in the Bible, in Numbers as it relates to the Levitical priesthood.

  So, if in fact you are a part of the tribe of Levi and engaged in the Levitical services of the Temple, then your retirement is biblical and you must obey this biblical directive. If you are not a Levitical priest serving in the Temple, then retirement may not be as biblical as some of us have surmised and imagined.

- Retirement is a relatively modern phenomenon.

  Great Depression and Social Security Act of 1935 (1935 – life expectancy was 61 years old).

- *The real issue at hand is not what to do in your retirement years, but instead to motivate you to make ready for that season of life so you will have the financial freedom to serve Christ in new and expanding ways post "retirement."*
- *Retooling rather than retiring. Help others during your "retirement" years.*

Chuck Bentley explains in the article "What Does the Bible Say About Retirement?"[11] (emphasis added)

- "God gave Adam work to do before the fall. Work is good."
- "We know work is good. Does that mean retirement is bad? The only mention of retirement found in the Bible is in Numbers 8:25 in reference to Levites. There is no other direction found in Scripture to suggest we should retire."
- "Retirement isn't necessarily sinful, but it does mean it should be viewed from a different perspective."
- "The problem with today's attitude towards retirement is that it completely negates an integral aspect of God's design – *that we were created to work.* It also normalizes something that was never intended to be normal – not working."
- "Retirement is not evil, wrong or bad." *Yet, retirement for Christians should mean freeing time to devote to serving others more fully without the necessity of getting paid for it. Time to repurpose how and why you invest time and resources.*

Billy Graham, who eventually retired from public preaching but served the Lord as long as he was able, once responded to a question from someone whose life goal was to retire at age fifty. Mr. Graham didn't condemn retirement, but he offered this insight:

- "Your goal ... suggests that you're only concerned about yourself. What will you do with the remaining years of your life, once you retire? Will you pursue a life of self-centered indulgence, living only for yourself? If so, you will end up restless, bored and empty. Instead, I urge you to put your life into God's hands by committing your life to Jesus Christ. Put Him at the center of your life, for only then will you find lasting joy and peace and satisfaction."

The cultural perspective of retirement, retiring to a self-centered life of leisure, is not biblical. The Bible does not directly reference the relatively new phenomenon of retirement, yet it does clearly state we are not to stop (or retire) our service to the Lord. The Bible is also clear that God created work and that work is good. Work doesn't have to be a job, or something we do for a paycheck. Work may be a vocation or something we are passionate about doing; paid or unpaid. Some people are blessed to have their work and vocation overlap. However, others may have a job that pays the bills and then engage in something outside of their job they are passionate about. From a biblical perspective, this vocation is to be based on service to others, not to self.

Retirement isn't necessarily biblical or non-biblical. It's largely dependent on your perspective and the intentional actions leading up to and through this life transition. This phase of life can, and should be, the most impactful and fulfilling phase because you're serving God through serving others.

Is your focus on you or on God?

Path Forward

So, what do you do? Do you work until you die? What if you're forced to retire from your job?

We all make several transitions throughout our life, including Renewalment. There is nothing wrong with transitioning to a new phase of life, and transitions are necessary. The problem arises when you transition to a self-centered life, making yourself your own god.

What might a biblical retirement transition look like? As with any life transition, it should be unique to the individual(s) transitioning, with one common denominator. The transition includes a focus on serving God through serving others, to His glory.

Through my personal experience, I discovered the need to step away from my own plan and instead seek God's plan for me. I was then able to discern God's plan; the one He designed in advance uniquely for me. It might seem like a subtle difference, yet it's a whole new mindset. And it's freeing. Reread this paragraph and reflect on your own unique situation.

This doesn't necessarily mean you will engage in a full-time job or vocation, but most likely that you'll find the blend of service, rest, and a job or vocation that best fits you. This blend can only be discovered in conversation between you and God. Discerning God's will for you comes from reading God's Word, through prayer and reflection, and wise counsel of others. (A discernment path is outlined later in the book.)

As noted by Chuck Bently, retirement is not evil, wrong, or bad. Yet, retirement for Christians should mean freeing time to devote to serving others more fully without the necessity of getting paid for it. Renewalment is a time to refocus, repurpose, and reposition why, where, and how you invest your time and resources.

As previously noted, I believe the word retirement itself is a hindrance. It has taken on a cultural view that basically suggests we should retire from our current life, and to delight in greener pastures where we will indulge ourselves until we grow old and die. You need a different outlook.

Bonnie and I prefer the word **Renewalment,** which indicates renewal. It's a refocusing, a repurposing, and a repositioning of how we steward what we've been entrusted with (time, talents, relationships, financial treasures, etc.) to serve God by serving others. We continually work the discernment path, finding the rhythm of service, rest, work, vocation, and structure that's right for us. It's an ongoing process. Through Renewalment, we're intentionally finding a life of provision, contentment, and enjoyment based on biblical principles. I'm not sure I've ever felt more spiritually fit, emotionally fit, relationally fit, and physically fit in unison than I do now in Renewalment. I'm providing value without necessarily having to be paid for my service.

My experience suggests the cultural worldview of retirement is not only unbiblical, it's dangerous to Christians and to non-Christians alike. A self-centered life can lead to all kinds of spiritual, emotional, relational, and physical problems. As Billy Graham said, "you will end up restless, bored, and empty."

As Mark Buchanan notes in his book, *The Rest of God: Restoring Your Soul by Restoring Sabbath[12]*:

"Any deep change in how we live begins with a deep change in how we think. The biblical word for this is repentance—in Greek, meta-noia, a change of mind. Repentance is a ruthless dismantling of old ways of seeing and thinking, and then a diligent and vigilant building of new ones."

Through my research, observation of others, and my personal experiences, I believe the key to thriving in this new phase of life centers around prayerfully and intentionally working through issues that inform your heart and perspective. These issues include your identity and purpose, values, and finding the rhythm that's right for you. We will focus on these areas throughout the rest of the book.

We'll guide you along your discovery path.

Take a few minutes right now to ponder and draft responses to the following questions...

- Is the focus of your life on you or God?
- Will you choose to listen to biblical wisdom (God's Word) or secular viewpoints?

- Do you have a flexible structure and process in place to be "diligent and vigilant?"

The human heart was designed for worship, and if it does not worship God, it will worship something else. That which we center our lives on can become our god. Will it be the tri-une-God or will it be something else? The Bible makes it clear you cannot worship both God and money (or any other man made idol that replaces God as your main focus in life).

- What will you choose to worship with your life?
- Will you choose your personal preferences or will you choose obedience to God's word?

Ron Blue helped me see the path to the heart for most humans is wrapped around money and possessions. Will you start to live into the five wise financial principles or not?

- Which of these five wise financial principles do you feel the best about?
- Which of these five wise financial principles do you have the least amount of confidence in?

"For where your treasure is, there your heart will be also." (Matthew 6:21 NIV)

Summary

Work

- Work is a gift from God, designed by and given by God. Work is good, even when it's frustrating.
- God designed each of us with our unique DNA, and each of us was made on purpose for a purpose. Each of us have been entrusted with individual spiritual gifts. God designed work and vocation for one's entire life, lived out in response to God's calling.
- This calling is not only for our time prior to retirement, it's meant for our entire life. Yes, what it looks like and how it is implemented will most likely change through the various life transitions and life phases we experience.

Leisure & Laziness

- The Bible makes two clear prohibitions...

  o Idleness... *"Slothfulness casts into a deep sleep, and an idle person will suffer hunger."* (Proverbs 19:15 ESV)
  o Self-Focused Pleasure... *"Or do you not know that your body is a temple of the Holy Spirit within you, whom you have from God? You are not your own, for you were bought with a price. So glorify God in your body."* (1 Corinthians 6:19-20 ESV)

- We are created for a purpose, on purpose, to make a difference no one else can. We are not called to a life of leisure, but to "do good." The primary evidence of what is in the heart is not words or emotions, but our deeds.

Lifestyle

- The Christian call is to live like Christ, and to strive to become more like Jesus.
- A 1 Timothy lifestyle is one of provision, contentment, and enjoyment.

Vocation (calling)

- We are here to love God and to love and serve other people.
- More than a job, it's a calling. It is a path for making a difference in the world beyond yourself and enjoy His presence forever.

Finances

- The only way to achieve your long-term financial goals is through the building of financial margin. This requires the incorporation of the 5 biblical financial principles into your daily routines, both as individuals and as a family.
- The key to building financial margin is to spend less than you earn, and to do it over a long period of time.

Retirement

- Cultural retirement (a life of leisure) is counter-intuitive to living for Christ.
- God calls us to service in this world throughout our entire life. He has a purpose in mind for us, before and during retirement. Your purpose to serve God through serving others never ends and never retires.
- A self-centered focus through a life of leisure leaves a big hole in your heart and in your soul. This is the reason for most of the disillusionment people have with retirement.
- Gratitude and serving others are the keys to thriving in Renewalment.
- The Christian never retires from Christ's service; they only change the address of their workplace. As one reaches "retirement age", the work/vocation may change but one's life work of serving the Lord does not change.
- One's older years are not to be spent solely in the pursuit of pleasure. Paul says the widow who lives for pleasure is dead while she yet lives (1 Timothy 5:6). Contrary to biblical instruction, many people equate retirement with the "pursuit of pleasure." That's not to say we can't/shouldn't enjoy golf, social functions, more time with family, and other pleasurable pursuits. Yet they should not be the primary focus of one's life at any age.
- The Renewalment phase of life can, and should be, your most impactful and fulfilling phase of life.

Chapter 3

HEART BELIEFS and PERSPECTIVES

Do you want to be obedient to God's Word, or not?

That's the real question of the heart. Information and knowledge are great, yet the wisdom of obedience is where the rubber meets the road.

> *"If anyone, then, knows the good they ought to do and doesn't do it, it is sin for them."* (James 4:17 NIV)

Are you willing to walk the walk? It's true that behavior follows belief. Is there anything you strongly believe in, but your behavior does not reflect that belief? I'm certain that has been true for every person at some point in their life. Why is that? Because for better or worse, we are creatures of habit. If our habits and routines don't change, our behavior won't change, no matter how much we want it to. Our daily habits often outweigh our best intentions.

The Habits Loop

As John Maxwell says, "You'll never change your life until you change something you do daily. The secret of your success is found in your daily routine."[1]

Change isn't always easy, even when we're convinced it's the right thing to do. You've probably heard that it takes up to thirty-one days of doing something new before it becomes a habit. While technically correct, I believe that is a little misleading.

As Charles Duhigg illustrates in his book *The Power of Habits*[2], habits are an outcome, not the change agent. He notes that habits are created by putting together a cue, a routine, and a reward. Then, we cultivate a craving (the why) that drives the loop. This leads to the habit.

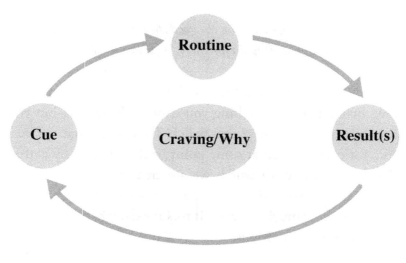

(The Habits Loop)

In order to put into practice what you believe in your heart, you will need to confirm your beliefs and commit to your desire to live them in your daily life. You will also need to be intentional about incorporating new routines into your daily life.

Do you want to be obedient to God's Word, or not?

If yes, are you willing to change and adjust a routine or two?

Personally, I wanted to honor our new stage of life called Renewalment. This included being more fit – spiritually, emotionally, relationally, and physically. While will-power is important, just focusing on sheer will-power for changing habits didn't help me. I needed to identify my why (craving), the cues, and new routines in order to reach the reward...an outcome of changed habits.

For example, I've always been fairly active, including at least thirty minutes of cardio workouts, periodic strength exercises, and yoga-type stretches. Yet, over time, through "portion distortion" and late-night snacking, I'd allowed myself to put on at least an extra twenty-five + pounds. For multiple years I attempted to change my eating habits through discipline and will-power. While both discipline and will-power are important, they are not enough. A focus on simply changing poor eating habits was not working. When I realized that habits are outcomes and not something I could directly change, it made all the difference! When I took the time to understand my poor eating cues and the subsequent routines that lead to a temporary reward resulting in a bad habit, I was able to recognize the cue and then use discipline and will-power to change the routine(s). This led to longer lasting rewards (e.g. feeling better, sleeping better, weight loss, more flexibility), with the new loop ending in the outcome of a new habit. As a bonus, I benefited from the outcome of losing more than twenty-five pounds and keeping it off for over a year.

When I asked myself the question, "Do you want to be obedient to God's Word?" I answered with a resounding, "Yes!" From then on, I knew I would need to adjust my daily routines. I wanted to be intentional about striving to become more like Jesus on a daily basis and to address life's issues and decisions with increased theological thinking. I wanted to become healthier spiritually, emotionally, relationally, and physically.

I made adjustments to my life by including three daily routines. For starters, I blocked off time first thing each morning to read and reflect on devotions and two chapters of the Bible, followed by prayers. Second, I committed time to intentionally exercise, including cardio, strength, and flexibility. Finally, I made a point each day to ask God for guidance, while building in time to pause and listen.

I also built some margin into my calendar throughout the day to prepare for meetings and to seek God's wisdom on how to bring value to those conversations in a respectful, loving, and truthful manner. My hope was to serve and add value for others. I trusted that by helping others, over time, the outcomes would work out for me. I hoped others would see God through my kind words, merciful acts, and wise advice.

Let me share a personal example of the importance of identifying cues in your daily life. Prior to my commitment to change my routine, I found myself raiding the food pantry in the evening when my wife Bonnie went to bed. This routine became my cue to indulge in unhealthy eating habits. In order to create a new habit loop, I developed a new routine in response to the cue of Bonnie going to bed. Instead of raiding the pantry, I added a simple yoga-type stretching routine. Throughout the day, I also entered what I ate into the LoseIt app to help manage portion distortion. These "minor" changes in my routine led to much more influential, powerful, and rewarding habits. As noted, the outcome has been a slow and steady weight loss of twenty-five pounds and keeping it off for more than a year. Yet the best outcome may be a better night of sleep.

It's important to identify the cues that signal appropriate routines. From there, you can identify the desired healthy outcome and why that change in routine leads to healthier habits. As a result, you'll discover that it could lead to weight loss, better health, energy, sleeping, and better overall functional fitness.

Be intentional, consistent, and work the habits loop. Identify your cues, routines, rewards, and clarity of the why (craving). Build your new routine into your weekly structure.

God Owns It All

> *"In the beginning, God created the heavens and the earth."* (Genesis 1:1 NIV)

"The earth is the Lord's and the fullness thereof,
the world and those who dwell therein."
(Psalm 24:1 ESV)

As noted by Mark Buchanan, "Any deep change in how we live begins with a deep change in how we think."[3] Our perspective, or how we think, leads to how we behave and act.

To change your perspective from, "this is all my stuff, all earned by me" to, "God owns it all, and I'm a steward of the money, possessions, work, relationships, and achievements," you must be intentional about this mindset shift. Your cultural environment is most likely working against this mindset. The culture tends to say, "It's all about you!" Is it time to change the environment you hang out in?

This perspective change will help you realize that it's not about you. It's about being a great steward with what God has entrusted you with. It's not about you and your achievements, it's about serving God through serving others in your current roles. It is about being content and at peace with what you have and where you are, yet not complacent. Your perspective will shift to working and serving as if working for the Lord, in excellence, and trusting in His outcome, no matter your role or job. It's relying on the multiplying power of the Holy Spirit to consistently grow your impact for God's kingdom, not your own "greatness."

"But seek first his kingdom and his righteousness,
and all these things will be given to you as well."
(Matthew 6:33 NIV)

We are stewards of what God has entrusted to us. Webster defines stewardship as "the activity or job of protecting and being responsible for something."

Building on that definition, I would suggest stewardship is the pursuit of God-given goals and objectives by using God-given resources such as our time, talents, relationships, and financial resources to the best of our ability.

You're called to be responsible for and protect what God has entrusted to you. Through the power of the Holy Spirit, you are to multiply what you've been entrusted with for the Kingdom (Parable of Talents).

One way or another, most of us have intentionally or unintentionally made money or possessions our idol. We need to realize that money is merely a tool. As Ron Blue says, money is "a tool, at test, and a testament," not the end goal. If you don't stop serving money, it will steal your contentment and joy. Scripture states, "For the love of money is the root of all kinds of evil" (1 Timothy 6:10). Money is not evil itself. It's just a tool to help you live your God-given plans. The trouble begins when we make money an idol. Love of money becomes the source of evil.

You can shift your perspective and allow money to serve as a means of provision, giving, joy, contentment, and vocation. Looking at Renewalment, it benefits you to rethink the question "How much money is enough?" when considering your Renewalment income, housing, cars, travel, and debt. You can start using money as the tool that allows you to fund your goals, your desired rhythm of service, rest, vocation, and structure both now and during Renewalment years. This allows you to be in a position to serve God during Renewalment without having to necessarily be paid. Your contentment will be fueled by moving away from a self-centered view of retirement and the never-ending need for more to a new life transition of impact and service for God's kingdom – a life of purpose, on purpose.

Do you believe God owns it all, and that you are called to steward for the kingdom what He has entrusted to your care?

Does your checkbook/credit card statement reflect this?

What changes do you need to make going forward?

The Christian Lifestyle

As previously noted, I believe 1 Timothy outlines the desired Christian lifestyle as provision, contentment, and enjoyment. God calls us to provide for our family, to be content with what He has entrusted us to steward, and to enjoy life. He calls us to live fully into our values so as to maximize our gifts and abilities. Within broad borders, we have a ton of liberty and choice.

What is provision? According to Webster it's "the art of or process of supplying or providing something; a supply of food and other things that are needed." Yes, you should provide for your family's physical needs. However, it's also critical to meet their emotional, relational, and spiritual needs. God promises to provide for our needs, and we are instructed to provide for the needs of our family. (1 Timothy 5:8)

When does our effort to provide result in hoarding? Can striving to provide become an idol of its own? First, only God can fully protect you. No amount of money or possessions can protect against all the ways we find ourselves derailed in life. You can use vehicles God has provided to do your best to shelter from hindrances to your family's possessions, health, income, and assets. It would be wrong not to do so. Yet no matter what you do, it can all be lost. Only God can protect. You can, however, find financial freedom, leaving you with financial choices. As you plan for future events such as Renewalment, you should ask the question, "How much is enough?" How much is enough to enable you to provide for your family, yet doesn't drift into the category of hoarding?

> *"A prudent person foresees danger and takes precautions. The simpleton goes blindly on and suffers the consequences."* (Proverbs 27:12 NLT)

"How much is enough?" This is actually a pretty loaded question! It encompasses many factors, including your individual perspective, emotions, anxiety, and spirituality. *However, the ways in which we use God's money should always reflect our spiritual perspective.* Couples need to be in open communication and find unity in the answer. This is a question to be addressed annually at the very least. In case you haven't noticed...life changes. The circumstances surrounding "how much is enough" will likely change as well.

To help find your answer to "How much is enough?" you need to be mindful of where you spend your money today. Track it on a pad of paper, a spreadsheet, or an online tool. It's impossible to develop financial margin and save for your priorities if you don't know how you're spending your money. Have you ever asked yourself, "Where does it all go?" Be sure to find out. Develop a realistic spending plan (not a "budget", but a plan for how you plan to spend the money God has entrusted to you aligned with your priorities), and then live by it. You do need discipline and a new routine to live within your spending plan. However, remember it's a plan, not law. Adjust the plan as you learn and then adjust your spending. Ensure open communication and unity in your decisions. It's most effective to live within a set range for your Spending Plan rather than a strict number.

As Ron Blue[4] notes, there are only five places to spend your money: giving, saving, taxes, debt repayment, and lifestyle. The appendix has an outline you can use to design your unique spending plan. Also keep in mind these five Wise Biblical Financial Principles to follow as you live into your spending plan:

1. Spend Less Than You Earn
2. Be Wise with Debt
3. Build Margin and Protect Yourself Against Setbacks
4. Have Short and Long Term Goals
5. Live Generously – Give Back

Knowing where you're currently spending the money God has entrusted you with, developing a spending plan for the future, living by the five wise biblical financial principles, and identifying your "enough" are essential steps. Always remember that the true answer to your question, "How much is enough?" can only be found on your knees in prayer. It's a math question with a spiritual answer.

"But godliness with contentment is great gain. For we brought nothing into the world, and we can take nothing out of it." (1 Timothy 6:6-7 NIV)

Contentment is about being at peace with what God has entrusted to you today. As noted earlier, if you're not content with what you have today, you will not be content with twice as much. As you learn to be content (yes it's a learned behavior), you are trusting that God knows what you need better than you do. He'll give you the wisdom to make good financial decisions, and to be a good steward. The Bible suggests that if you're not trustworthy with what you've been given, why should you expect more? (Luke 16:10-12)

"Whoever can be trusted with very little can also be trusted with much, and whoever is dishonest with very little will also be dishonest with much." (Luke 16:10 NIV)

If you're not satisfied with what you have today, you will not be satisfied with more. When asked how much it takes to be happy, billionaire Howard Hughes reportedly said, "Just a little more." If you're never satisfied, you'll never find contentment and you'll always want more. It's a downward-spiraling catch-22 leading to frustration, anxiety, fear, and a lack of joy in your life.

To be clear, being content is to be satisfied with what God has entrusted you to steward. It does not mean you should be complacent or lazy. Contentment is being satisfied and happy with what has been entrusted to you as you seek to multiply these resources for God's kingdom in a God-pleasing manner. The opposite of contentment is being complacent, and accepting the status quo with little effort to make improvements. We are to find contentment in what the Lord has entrusted to us, yet we are not to be satisfied with our current state. We are to grow, improve, and share the resources we've been given. The Parable of Talents (Matthew 25:14-30) is clear on God's expectation that we put the resources He has blessed us with to work for the Kingdom. Jesus shows us a better way.

In his article *Contentment: Found or Lost*[5], Dr. David Jeremiah shares the following insights on contentment:

> Let's face it — it's a challenge to remain content these days. Physically, we know we're not one of the "beautiful people" (but would love to be). Emotionally, we live lives of stress, hard work, dirty diapers, and bills to pay (but wish we didn't). Materially, we're afraid we're never going to "move on up to the East side and finally get our piece of the pie" (but wish we would). And spiritually, we feel guilty for not being satisfied physically, emotionally, or materially. It's a vicious circle.

> I'm not rehearsing the evidence of our discontent to make us feel bad. I'm doing it to point us in the direction of true contentment.

> **Contentment is...**

> I believe the most complete passage in Scripture on this subject is Philippians 4:10-20. The

amazing reality about this passage on contentment is that Paul wrote it while in prison for his faith. Here's his key thought: *"...I have learned in whatever state I am, to be content...[for] my God shall supply all your needs according to His riches in glory by Christ Jesus."* (Philippians 4:11, 19 NKJV)

1. Contentment is learned behavior.
2. Contentment is not dependent on circumstances.
3. Contentment is a state of being, not a state of doing.
4. Contentment is based on the riches of God in Christ Jesus.

There's nothing wrong with possessing things. But there is something wrong if we can't be content without them. May God speak to your heart and help you seek, and find, contentment in **Him.**

"But godliness with contentment is great gain. For we brought nothing into the world, and we can take nothing out of it." (1 Timothy 6:6-7 NIV)

As mentioned, contentment is a learned behavior. God is more interested in your character than your comfort. He wants you to grow and become more like Jesus. As Rick Warren says, "When you learn to be content, you are believing that God knows what you need better than you do and trusting that he will give you the necessary wisdom to make good financial decisions."

Contentment does not come naturally. It's something we need to intentionally practice daily. It must be a part of your daily routine. If you don't learn to be comfortably content, you'll always want more. That continuous wanting will lead to discontentment, anxiety, frustration, and stress.

As Tony Dungy notes in *The One Year Uncommon Life Daily Challenge,* "Contentment is possible when you start with a grateful heart. Not a token sense of gratitude, but the realization that the Lord has blessed you with everything you need. Notice the difference? The first approach says that something is missing in our lives and we need to get it... The moment you size up what you own or have accomplished, often it's only a short leap to feeling that you've been shortchanged. A contented life is achieved when you focus on what God has given you and thank Him for these blessings."

Enjoyment is part of God's plan for each of us, but what is joy? Most of us think of it as emotional happiness. However, happiness is a fleeting emotion dependent on our situation and outside circumstances. True joy is a Jesus centered confidence, believing he is who he says he is and that you are who he says you are.

Webster defines joy as "the emotion evoked by well-being, success, or good fortune or by the prospect of possessing what one desires." This definition leaves something lacking, never able to be fulfilled.

Theopedia describes joy as "a state of mind and an orientation of the heart. It is a settled state of contentment, confidence, and hope...Christians should always find reasons to be joyful. There are many ways to define joy. Joy isn't just a smile or a laugh. Joy is something that is deep within and doesn't leave quickly. When we have the joy of the Lord, we'll know it and so will others. Since joy is given by God and something that He wants us to have, we need to be joyful! In addition to being joyful, we should let others have their joy and not bring them down when they are excited about good things. *The only thing worse than not having joy is stealing someone else's."*

This is a more convincing description of joy and where we find true joy, well beyond the fleeting emotion of happiness. Personally, I've found it impactful to intentionally pause peri-odically throughout the day to find that state of mind – an orientation of the heart through gratitude and joy. Recently, I've found the use of "The One Minute" app based on John Eldredge's book *Get Your Life Back*, and its notifications to be a helpful reminder to take an intentional pause.

The Bible has a lot to say about finding true joy:

> *Nehemiah said, "Go and enjoy choice food and sweet drinks, and send some to those who have nothing prepared. This day is holy to our Lord. Do not grieve, for the joy of the Lord is your strength."* (Nehemiah 8:10 NIV)

> *"Fill my heart with joy when their grain and new wine abound."* (Psalm 4:7 NIV)

> *"You make known to me the path of life you will fill me with joy in your presence with eternal pleasures at your right hand."* (Psalm 16:11 NIV)

"With joy you will draw water from the wells of salvation." (Isaiah 12:3 NIV)

"The kingdom of heaven is like treasure hidden in a field. When a man found it, he hid it again, and then in his joy went and sold all he had and bought that field." (Matthew 13:44 NIV)

"I have told you this so that my joy may be in you and that your joy may be complete." (John 15:11 NIV)

True joy comes from a relationship with God the Father (Creator), Jesus Christ the Son (Savior) and the Holy Spirit (Helper).

An excerpt from *Whisper: How to Hear the Voice of God*[7] by Mark Batterson (emphasis added):

"Seven times in the book of Genesis, God steps back from the canvas of His creation and admires His handiwork and sees that it is good. It's the Almighty's first reaction to His creation. It's the first recorded emotion that God expresses.

The word good comes from the Hebrew word tob. It's joy unspeakable. It's pure delight. That first emotion sets the tone, sets the bar. God delights in what He does, and He wants nothing less for us. He wants us to delight in His creation. He wants us to delight in one another. And above all, He wants us to delight ourselves in Him.

"Man's chief end is to glorify God, and to enjoy him forever."

Tell me how much you enjoy God, and I'll tell you how spiritually mature you are.

In the Sermon on the Mount, Jesus revealed a supernatural sequence that is inviolable. He said, "Seek first his kingdom and his righteousness, and all these things will be given to you as well."

Seeking God first is delighting yourself in the Lord. Seeking God first is giving Him the first word and the last word. Seeking God first is making sure His voice is the loudest voice in your life.

In the apostle Paul's words, "I consider everything a loss because of the surpassing worth of knowing Christ Jesus my Lord." (Philippians 3:8 ESV) Then and only then will God speak to us in the language of desires. He'll change our desires, intensify our desires, and upload new desires within us. Those desires actually become spiritual compasses by which we navigate the will of God.

And some thoughts from a compellingtruth.org article *What is God's view of pleasure? Is He opposed to pleasure?...*

"Some people view God's commands in Scripture as a way of life that opposes pleasure. He is not

opposed to pleasure; He is opposed to sinning
to experience pleasure.

Ultimately, we have been created to find our
greatest pleasure in God Himself. Psalm 37:4
teaches, *Delight yourself in the Lord, and he will
give you the desire of your heart.* When we walk
closely to the Lord, we find the most pleasure,
not the least pleasure. God is not opposed to
pleasure. He instead knows that the best for us
is found in our complete devotion to Him."[8]

God wants us to have a life of provision, contentment, and
enjoyment. Enjoy the Lord and enjoy all the things He has
provided for us: family, food, scenery, relationships, careers, the
church, recreation, and houses just to name a few – without
making them into your god instead of our Lord and Savior.

Enjoy your lifestyle. When you get to heaven, God isn't going
to compare you with anyone else, but he will compare you with
yourself. What did you do with what you were given? What are
you doing with what you've been entrusted with?

*Jesus, may I always seek your will first as I determine how to
steward the possessions and resources you have graciously given me
to steward. Amen.*

Personally, my starting point was the realization, internaliza-
tion, and implementation of the fact that God owns it all. I
had to move beyond the logic (head knowledge) of this fact to
a true heart-felt and spiritual belief and application. I had to

acknowledge that God has blessed me with what I need, and that my role is to be a great steward of all the resources God has entrusted to me. I'm learning to be satisfied and content with the amount I've been entrusted with, and perhaps most importantly, I'm learning not to compare my own resources to what others have. I'm realizing I can be content yet not complacent, always looking to grow personally, especially striving to mature as a follower of Jesus. These mindsets and behaviors helped lead to enjoying life, and provided a more relaxed focus on serving instead of getting. It's all a work in progress, one step at a time, and there is no perfection to it. It's simply continually growing and maturing as a follower of Jesus.

Path Forward

Before moving to chapter 4, take time to answer the following questions. Yes, there are several questions, but answering the questions for yourself will help clarify your core perspectives as you strive to thrive in Renewalment. (Perspectives/beliefs lead behavior.)

The Habits Loop

- Do you want to be obedient to God's Word, or not?
- If yes, are you willing to change/adjust a routine or two?

  o   Identify and write down the perspectives or mindsets you want to change.

- What's your "why"? (Identify and document your why for change. When your why is strong enough, then you can focus on and implement the how.)
- What are the routines you need to change, delete, or add to live into your desired mindsets?

  o Gain clarity of these routines, along with the cues, cravings, and rewards – then intentionally work the new routines.

God Owns It All

- Do you believe God Owns It All? Really?
- Does your behavior convict you of this belief?
- Identify and document your key beliefs. (Remember behavior follows belief.)

  o Do you believe you are called to steward what He has entrusted to your care?
  o What are your key beliefs about retirement?
  o What are your key beliefs about biblical financial principles?

- What needs to change in how you approach "your stuff?"
- Are you chasing false gods or idols (e.g. money, career, etc.)? Do your actions suggest you believe it's all up to you?
- With a renewed mindset and perspective, what new habit loops do you need to work on?

Christian Lifestyle

- What are your key beliefs about the Christian lifestyle for you? (Remember behavior follows belief.)
- How do you define what provision, contentment, and enjoyment look like to you? (Be on your knees for guidance.)
- How do you plan to start to live into the 5 wise biblical financial principles?
- How do you need to reprioritize your calendar and checkbook (credit card charges)?

<u>Summary</u>

The Habits Loop

- As John Maxwell says, "You'll never change your life until you change something you do daily. The secret of your success is found in your daily routine."
- Do you want to be obedient to God's Word, or not? If yes, are you willing to change/adjust a routine or two?
- Creating a new habit is an outcome; the process and the key to change is within the cue, the routine, the result, and the driving "why".

God Owns It All

- Change your mindset from "I own all this stuff, it's mine", to the truth that God owns it all and has entrusted you to be a steward of it.
- The only parts of the Bible you truly believe are the parts you put into practice. If what you say you believe doesn't change how you live your life, then you probably

don't really believe it. What do you truly believe? Are you living your beliefs?

- How will a change in perspective change how your calendar and checkbook (credit card account) look?

Lifestyle

- Provide for your immediate and extended family.
- Intentionally seek contentment. It's not necessarily natural, but true contentment is found in a relationship with Jesus Christ. Contentment is a learned behavior; it's a state of being, not of doing.
- Enjoyment is part of God's plan for us. Joy is given by God and is something He wants you to have. Enjoyment is a Jesus-centered confidence. Seek it!

Chapter 4

IDENTITY, CORE VALUES and PURPOSE

Where Do We Find Our Identity?

MERRIAM-WEBSTER DEFINES IDENTITY as "the distinguishing character or personality of an individual." A person's identity describes who someone is, including the qualities and beliefs that make a particular person or group different from others.

Your personal identity is the way you see yourself or would like to see yourself and is closely related to your self-image. How you see yourself will affect the way you feel about yourself and how you behave in challenging situations (e.g. a transition from full-time employment). Where do you find your identity?

A 2018 LifeWay research project titled "Where Americans Find Their Identity?"[1] asked Americans, "When you think about who you are, what are the first three things that come to mind?" As an open-ended question, the responses were:

- Parent. 25%
- Intelligent. 12%
- Job. 11%
- Compassionate. 11%
- Christian. 8%
- Religious/Spiritual. 2%

When given a list of potential facets that could be "very important" in their identity, they selected:

- My Role in My Family. 73%
- The Good I Do. 57%.
- What I Have Achieved. 51%
- My Role as a Friend. 49%
- My Interests or Hobbies. 44%
- What I Have Endured. 39%
- My Religious Faith. 37%

These are all good things, yet they may be inconsistent or frequently change. **Any time you base your identity on changing factors, it's as if you're building on shifting sand. You are setting yourself up for failure and disappointment.**

When you lose your identity, you start to lose your self-image. Your behavior becomes less than constructive, and life can spiral downhill. Having a firm grasp on your identity (who you are and who you want to be) is critical to finding a life of provision, contentment, and enjoyment. It's essential to thriving in Renewalment. You need to gain clarity of your identity before, during, and after the Renewalment life transition.

When Americans were asked which statement best described their opinion, they responded:

- What I Do Determines Who I Am. 42%
- Who I Am Determines What I Do. 42%
- Not Sure. 15%

There is no single identifier that accurately reflects what Americans think of themselves. For most people, their identity and self-value is based on ever-changing outside influences that are outside of their control. This is a formula for disaster.

I've seen many retirees experience a loss of their identity. "Who am I now that I'm not the plumber, banker, VP, boss, or owner?" The way you see yourself is closely related to your self-image. So when people lose their identity, they also lack clarity surrounding their sense of direction and purpose. They start to ask questions like…

Now that I'm retired, do I have value? Am I relevant?

If you don't know who you are, how are you supposed to know how you should act and behave? How do you find contentment and enjoyment? The answer is: you don't.

Many retirees look for their identity in other people, their possessions, accomplishments, or hobbies. When you look for your identity in outside sources, you're only setting yourself up for disappointment.

This lack of identity can lead to some very unhealthy behaviors and habits such as overeating, a sedentary lifestyle, smoking, too much time alone, relying on pain medication, or drinking too much alcohol. (HomeCare Assistance[2] article). An unhealthy lifestyle can also greatly enhance the risk of disability (HealthDay[3] article). Searching for identity from an ever changing world view is a dangerous path, and almost certainly leads to disillusionment. So where do you find a never changing, rock-solid foundation for your identity? It's in the one transcendent, always true, never changing reality: the Bible.

What does the Bible have to say about our identity?

- You are created in God's image. (Genesis 1:27)
- You are created with a plan – a future and a hope. (Jeremiah 29:11)
- You are created as a Child of God. (1 John 3:1-3)
- You are created as heirs. (Romans 8:17)
- You are created for good works. (Ephesians 2:10)
- You are created as part of the body of Christ. (1 Corinthians 12: 27)
- You are created as temples of the Holy Spirit. (1 Corinthians 6:19-20)
- You are chosen by God. (John 15:16)
- You are saved by grace. (Ephesians 2:4-5)
- You are created to be ambassadors for Christ. (2 Corinthians 5:20)

Wow! Now *that* is an everlasting identity, no matter what happens around you. Be assured that you were made on purpose and for a purpose. You have immense value. You are a deeply loved child of God and an heir of Jesus. Powerful!

How would believing the truth about your identity in Christ change the way you see yourself, how you live, and your self-worth no matter the outside circumstances?

The only way to know your true identity (who you are) and what your purpose is in life is to look to God. Why? Because he created you! He created you on purpose for a purpose.

It's critical to take time to work through your identity, especially in this new transition and phase of life. You are a child of God. As a child of God, you have built-in worth and hope in life eternal. Your past has been forgiven and forgotten, you have purpose for the present, and you have hope for the future. Do you believe this? Take a minute to pause and confirm this truth. Remember, your behavior follows your beliefs.

> *"Do not conform to the pattern of this world, but be transformed by the renewing of your mind. Then you will be able to test and approve what God's will is – his good, pleasing and perfect will."* (Romans 12:2 NIV)

As a child of God, how do you want to show up day-to-day? How do you want to be seen by others, including your family? When it comes to family and those close to you, more tends to be caught through observation and conversations with you than anything you could ever teach directly. In many instances, your daily life may be the only interpretation of the Bible others will ever be exposed to. Are they witnessing and observing the Truth through your behavior?

If you don't clarify your identity and values, your behavior tends to be incongruent with how you see yourself, either consciously or subconsciously. If you don't have clarity of your identity and values, you will tend to have internal dissonance. This can lead to anxiety, stress, fear, or depression. But it is avoidable!

Be intentional, take the time to ask yourself the identity and life values questions outlined at the end of this section, and then live out your answers. Set a task to periodically review how you are doing and how your new learnings should impact your behavior.

We have all been designed with a God-sized hole in our heart, and it can only be filled through an ongoing relationship with Jesus. We can attempt to fill it with work, family, medicating, and busyness, yet none of those things will be fulfilling over the long haul. You find your true identity and purpose through a living relationship with Jesus. It's the only way you can permanently fill the God-sized hole in your heart. Other things such as work, worry, booze, pills, sex, or hobbies might seem to fill the hole temporarily, yet they will just lead to a bigger and deeper hole.

Know your identity in Christ, clarify and live your core values, and then intentionally live a Christ-centered life through your chosen vocation.

It's also important to realize that the quality and depth of your "vertical" relationships with family and friends will not be stronger than your vertical relationship with God.

Your identity and your life purpose need to align to achieve congruence and contentment. In his research article titled *Purpose is Key to Third Third Flourishing*[4], Mark Roberts points out...

> "We often think of finding a purpose in life as something young adults need to do. It's crucial for folks in their late teens and twenties to identify their purpose so that they might live meaningful and productive lives.
>
> Though I certainly agree that young adults need to find a purpose worth living for, I have come to believe that purpose is essential, not only for Millennials and Gen Z folk, but also for those of us entering the third third of life. We need a clear purpose so that we might flourish as we get older, experiencing personal wellbeing and making a difference that matters in the world.
>
> As it turns out, purpose not only enriches the third third of life. It also extends it. Older adults who have a purpose live better and longer. That's what serious scholarly research reveals."

God didn't create anything without a purpose. If you're breathing, you have a purpose. In Christ, you have something to offer the world. You are God's masterpiece. Before you were born, God planned the good things he wanted you to do with your entire life. What you do matters throughout your whole life, not just during your "working" years.

As you approach or enter Renewalment, I truly believe you are in the prime of your life. Don't laugh! You have unique life experiences, and you've managed your way through the ups and downs of life. You are in a prime position to help others grow, give back, serve, and to make the difference you've always wanted to make. Now is the time. Be you, be present, be intentional and consistent, and adjust as you learn. Who you are and what you do matters! Only you can fill the puzzle piece God designed uniquely for you.

I'll offer an example. My identity is defined as "a child of God and a joint heir with Jesus." My life values are to love, serve, and grow. I want to love God and my neighbor, serve others, act like Jesus, and continually mature as a Jesus follower. This is not profound, yet it's who I want to be and I'm working to intentionally live it out in my daily life.

To help you articulate your **identity,** respond to the following questions. Write down your first thoughts, and don't overthink it:

- What are you?
- Who do you believe you are or would like to become?
- What is your self-worth based on?
- Whose are you?
- Who do you want to be seen as and known for by your parents, spouse, friends, peers, kids, and grandkids?
- Do you want to determine your identity on changing factors (shifting sand) or on a rock-solid foundation?
- Review the above list. What are the common themes?

Now use the common themes to draft an "identity statement" in one to three sentences.

What Are Your Core Values?

Your core life values strongly influence your identity and how you show up day-to-day. Are you living your life values? Do you even know what your values are? My experience is that most people would answer that question with a "yes," yet they have not taken the time to clearly think about what their values are and have not written them down.

Values are stable, long-lasting beliefs about what is important to a person. They become standards by which people order their lives and make their choices. A belief tends to develop into a value when the person's commitment to it grows and they see it as being important.

Once you have clarified your core life values and have written them down, it becomes easier to intentionally and consistently live them. As you live according to your key life values, you will also start to grow into who you want to be. Then you can start to live into your true identity. Alignment of your values and your identity will help lead to alignment with your behavior. This is critical for overall congruence, contentment and peace of mind.

To help you articulate your **core values**, respond to the following questions. Write down your first thoughts. Don't overthink it and don't prejudge, simply write down what comes to mind.

- What are the values you desire to live by?
- What's important to you in life?
- If you could have any career, without worrying about money or other practical constraints, what would you do?

- When you're reading news stories, what sort of story or behavior tends to inspire you?
- What type of story or behavior makes you angry?
- What do you want to change about the world or about yourself?
- What are you most proud of?
- When are you the happiest?

Review and consolidate your lists, and identify common themes. Then prioritize the list and identify your top three to five life values you want to ensure you'll be living.

Where Do We Find Purpose?

Merriam-Webster defines purpose as:

- The reason why something is done or used: the aim or intention of something.
- The feeling of being determined to do or achieve something
- The aim or goal of a person: what a person is trying to do, become, etc.
- Something set up as an objective or end to be attained.

A few synonyms for purpose are motive, motivation, grounds, cause, impetus, occasion, and reason.

According to a 2018 Pew Research Center[5] study, Americans are most likely to mention family when describing what provides them with a sense of meaning. In an open-ended question, the percentage of Americans who describe what provides them with a sense of meaning is as follows...

Family	69%
Career	34%
Money	23%
Spirituality & faith	20%
Friends	19%
Activities and hobbies	19%
Health	16%
Home & surroundings	13%
Learning	11%

In closed-ended questions (i.e. given a list to choose from), the percentage of Americans who describe a specific source of meaning and fulfillment in their lives is as follows:

… is the MOST… provides a

important source. "great deal"

Spending time with family	40%	69%
Being outdoors	5%	47%
Spending time with friends	4%	47%
Caring for pets	6%	45%
Listening to music	3%	44%
Reading	2%	37%
Your religious faith	20%	36%
Your job or career	4%	34%

All of the items above are good things, yet they are also based on things that will change and will most likely disappoint you at some point. Having your sense of meaning or purpose in life based on things that continuously ebb and flow with the environment and circumstances means your sense of purpose and value will also ebb and flow. It will always be on shifting sand. Instead of building your sense of purpose and value on shifting sand, perhaps it is better to build it on a rock-solid foundation of Biblical principles.

Purpose is understanding why you do what you do. It's what drives your energy, motivation, and behavior. Purpose gives you meaning and direction. Without a clear purpose we wither away. God made us on purpose and for a clear purpose – to love God and our neighbor, to serve God through serving others, and to share the Good News.

A few of the things the Bible says about purpose:

- "Go and make disciples of all nations and teach and share with them the Good News of salvation." (Matthew 28:19-20)
- "...Fear God and keep his commandments, for this is the duty of all mankind." (Ecclesiastes 12:13 NIV)
- "Be transformed by the renewing of your mind; discern God's will." (Romans 12:2)
- "Whatever you do, do it for the glory of God and not to your own glory." (1 Corinthians 10:31)
- "Seek first his kingdom and his righteousness..." (Matthew 6:33 NIV)
- "Do the good works prepared in advance for you." (Ephesians 2:10)
- "Love God and love your neighbor. There are no commandments greater than these." (Mark 12:30-3)

- "...To act justly and to love mercy and to walk humbly with your God." (Micah 6:8 NIV)
- "Use your gifts to serve one another." (1 Peter 4:10)
- "Multiply through the power of Christ." (Ephesians 3:20)
- "Trust the Lord, not your own understanding." (Proverbs 3:5)

"Do you want to know what God's will is for you? It is for you to become more and more like Christ. This is spiritual maturity, and if you make this your goal, it will change your life."[6] – Billy Graham

Rick Warren (Saddleback Church) outlines and simplifies Five Eternal Life Purposes[7] that universally apply to each of us. He says God has given each of us the following five life purposes:

1. To know and to love God. (Worship)
2. To learn to love others. (Fellowship)
3. To grow spiritually and become more like Jesus. (Discipleship)
4. To serve God by serving others. (Ministry)
5. To share the Good News with others. (Outreach)

When you find your identity in Christ, you're going to find your purpose and the motivation needed to get to work on your purpose, with purpose, and with energy.

The five purposes identified above are what I call "macro-purposes", and they are universal for all of us. They are a pathway for living into a 24/7 Christ-like lifestyle focused on personal identity, purpose, and fulfillment centered on a rock-solid foundation of biblical principles. These lead to a life of contentment, fulfillment, and enjoyment.

How we go about implementing these five purposes and the environment we do it within is unique for each of us, and we must be intentional and consistent in how we live into these five eternal life purposes in our daily life. Please note the five purposes are not a list of things to check off as you complete them. They are to be lived throughout your life, with God at the center of everything you do, no matter what your job or vocation is.

There are numerous, perhaps unlimited, ways for each of us to live out the 5 macro-purposes we are designed for. The various ways we can live out these purposes through our vocation or calling are unique to each of us based on our experiences, spiritual gifts, talents, passions, relationships, abilities, and opportunity.

My friend, Rev. Dr. Doug Hill, defines purpose as "how you feel you are called to pursue life for yourself and others." From my perspective, this is the definition of what I call your "micro-purpose," or your day-to-day calling.

While the five macro-purposes are the same for each of us throughout our life, our *micro*-purpose(s) might change through life transitions and people, or situations God entrusts to our care. As you live out your purposes through your work and/or vocation (calling) and transition into Renewalment, it's important to remain dynamic and flexible. Continue to adjust as you learn by finding a good blend of work/vocation (calling), rest/vacation, and service/giving back. You'll need a plan and structure to make intentional forward progress. You'll also need to be flexible in order to implement what you learn and adjust life events to align with your priorities.

Purpose is critical for our Renewalment years. Keep in mind that God is less concerned with what you do as a Renewalment vocation and more focused on who you become and who you do it for. It's critical to be intentional and consistent about how you daily live out your God ordained purposes through a structure for your chosen vocation. (More on structure later.)

For most people, vocation tends to be the intersection of skills or spiritual gifts, God-given passions, and areas that meet the needs of other people. It's important to take the time to identify your Renewalment vocation. From there, you can determine how it might be aligned with your micro-purpose(s) and how you will live into the five eternal purposes. You can't just expect your vocation to materialize. You must intentionally discern what it is or might be.

Don't overcomplicate it. Make a list to identify your strengths, spiritual gifts, passions, and needs in the marketplace. Seek out roles (paid or unpaid) that best fit this intersection, and then act! You're looking for a good fit, not a perfect one. If it doesn't work out, learn from it and move forward into living the five eternal purposes, intentionally and consistently.

> *"The place God calls you to is where your deep gladness and the world's deep hunger meet."[8]*
> -Fredrick Buechner

The following questions might also help you find and clarify your personal purpose:

- What am I on this earth for, and why do I exist?
- What do I like to do?
- Who do I want to help?
- What do I want to see changed or accomplished?
- Looking at my identity statement, what do I see as my calling?

Review and consolidate your responses as appropriate. Identify the common themes and draft your "purpose statement" into one to three sentences. Remember that while identifying your purpose is critical, God is less concerned with what you do as a vocation and is more focused on who you become and who you do it for.

Gaining clarity of your identity, core life values, and purpose will help determine how you'll live into your purposes for God's glory. This is the only way to truly find joy, fulfillment, and contentment and to thrive in Renewalment.

The Importance of Structure

In order to live into your desired identity, life values, and purpose you'll need to ensure you have a **structure** in place that works for you. Without a flexible yet intentional structure, you'll flounder.

Many enter retirement with a "go-with-the-flow" attitude, which is understandable. However, this could become a huge problem. We need structure in our lives. A lack of structure fuels anxiety. Of course, the structure should be more flexible and relaxed than during your years spent as a full-time employee. But, planning your daily and weekly structure is essential for this new season of life. You need a structure that helps you settle into a rhythm that fits your purpose, combines your skills and calling, and provides opportunities to serve others and give back.

Structure is critical for the intentional consistency needed to thrive in Renewalment. Without it, you're in a perpetual state of cognitive dissonance that fuels your anxiety and discontentment. You need a daily and weekly structure that works for you, and one that allows for making adjustments as you learn. This is what I call a "Rhythm Week".

In our personal Rhythm Week, Bonnie and I intentionally and consistently plan at least a week ahead in order to build our priorities into our routine. This way we are living our overarching purpose to love and serve God by loving and serving others. We daily ask, "God, what would you have me do today?" and then listen and respond in obedience. (No, we don't do this perfectly, yet to the best of our ability. Then we learn, adjust, and grow forward.) We're finding the rhythm that works for us to determine our own blend of vocation, rest, and service, and giving back.

> *God, may everything I do today – every decision,*
> *every interaction, every word, every deed – be a*
> *seed for your kingdom. Amen.*

Because my life-plan coaching is built on a foundation of biblical principles, I am able to help individuals and couples gain clarity when approaching or entering Renewalment. I help them clarify their identity, life values, priorities, and purpose with an eternal and long-term focus. This provides a freeing experience, greatly reducing anxiety and stress, and provides a path to thrive in Renewalment in their own unique way. This is accomplished through an intentional prioritization process, with weekly structure for follow-through. It's crucial to be intentional about living out priorities and flexibility as life happens.

The Bible is a sure foundation on which to base our lives and decisions.

> *"I will instruct you and teach you in the way you should go; I will counsel you with my loving eye on you."* (Psalm 32:8 NIV)

Without intentionally and consistently structuring your routines, you will find yourself aimlessly floating through life while lacking contentment, fulfillment, and enjoyment. You're much more likely to arrive at your desired destination if you're intentional about where you're headed and devise a plan for how to get there.

We will discuss the "how" of structure in more detail in Chapter 7 of this book.

Path Forward

Gain clarity of your identity.

- Who are you?

- Who would you like to become?
- On what do you base your self-worth?
- Whose are you?
- Who do you want to be seen as and known for by your kids, grandkids, parents, and friends?
- Write an "identity statement" in one to three sentences.

Gain clarity of your core life values.

- What's important to you in life?
- Take three minutes and write down all the values you'd like to live by.
- Review and consolidate your list as appropriate. Identify your top three to five life values you want to ensure you'll be living.

Gain clarity of your micro-purpose(s).

- What are you on this earth for, and why do you exist?
- What do you see as your calling for living into your identity?
- What do you like to do?
- Who do you want to help?
- What do you want to see changed or accomplished in your life?
- Write a "purpose statement" in one to three sentences.

The Importance of Structure

- Live your identity, life values, and your purpose through the development of your unique Rhythm Week. (The "what" and the "how" of the Rhythm Week is outlined in Chapter 7).

How will clarifying and documenting your identity, life values, and purpose from a biblical perspective impact your well-being?

<u>Summary</u>

Renewalment is a renewing, refocusing, and repositioning of where you invest the resources God has entrusted to your care. This includes your time, experiences, relationships, energy, spiritual gifts, talents, abilities, insights, money, and possessions. Everyone's experience with Renewalment is unique and based on individual identity, life values, purpose(s), and priorities. A key to living a life of provision, contentment, and enjoyment in Renewalment is to be purposeful, intentional, and consistent and to build margin on a day-to-day basis. This requires developing a structure that fits you.

The truth is that God owns it all. I believe the "job to be done" for each of us is to be a great steward of what God has entrusted to our care – our relationships, networks, spiritual gifts, talents, resources, and finances – as we live out God's plan for our life, strive to be more like Jesus, and as we prepare for eternal life in heaven.

No one will perfectly live and thrive in Renewalment. The goal is not to be perfect, but to be faithful. It is easier to make a course correction to a plan already set in motion than one that hasn't started or is haphazard at best, bouncing around based on the environment and what other people think. A go-with-the-flow plan will lead to an unfulfilled life lacking contentment and joy, leading to disillusionment and disappointment.

To help thrive in Renewalment and to help you make appropriate course corrections ensure you have clarity of your identity, your core values, your purpose, and a flexible structure to intentionally live them.

Where Do You Find Your Identity?

- Most Americans find their identity in things that change and will most likely go away all together. This leaves them to wonder who they are and what their values are. It's a depressing thought.
- When you lose your identity, you start to lose your self-image and your behavior becomes less constructive.
- Your life values strongly influence your identity and how you show up day-to-day. Are you living your life values? Do you even know what your values are?
- The only rock-solid place to find your identity is in God – as a child of God, and as an heir with eternal life.

What Are Your Core Life Values?

- Your core values also strongly influence your identity.
- Most people have not clarified their core values, and they definitely haven't written them down.
- Without clarity of your values, your behavior tends to be incongruent with what you desire.

Where Do You Find Purpose?

- Most people find their purpose in things that will change and will most likely disappoint them at some point.
- Purpose is understanding why you do what you do and is a key self-motivator for how you feel you are called to pursue life for yourself and others.
- Purpose gives you meaning and direction. Without a clear purpose, we wither away.
- God made you on purpose, for a purpose. There are five eternal God-given life macro-purposes.
- You can intentionally and consistently live into these five macro-purposes as part of a 24/7 Christ-like life-style through your unique God-given micro-purpose(s) to find a life of contentment, fulfillment, and enjoyment.

The Importance of Structure

- Without an intentional and consistent structure to live your unique routines, you will find yourself aimlessly floating through life, lacking contentment, fulfillment, and enjoyment.
- You're much more likely to arrive at your desired destination if you're intentional about where you're headed and devise a plan for how to get there.

Chapter 5

INCOME OPPORTUNITIES

GOD HAS NO issue with you having money. The problem comes when money has you.

> *"For the love of money is a root of all kinds of evil. Some people, eager for money, have wandered from the faith and pierced themselves with many griefs."*
> (1 Timothy 6:10 NIV)

Retirement Income

It's important to establish your life's purpose with a rock-solid biblical foundation. Otherwise you will not thrive in Renewalment regardless of the amount of money in your bank account. Once you've secured a strong foundation, you do need a monthly Renewalment "paycheck" to live out your life priorities. I believe a freeing part of Renewalment is being in a financial position where you can serve the Lord without necessarily having to be paid. You may choose to be paid, yet it does not have to be at the going rate, or even at all.

You're now ready to discuss financial freedom (remember it's financial "freedom", not financial "security" – only God can provide security). Financial freedom is being in a financial position to have freedom of choice, and to have positive financial options when life happens.

Whether you are just transitioning into Renewalment, preparing for Renewalment, or are already there, the financial focus needs to be on your retirement *income*. During the five years prior to this life transition, it's important to shift your focus on asset accumulation to align with your anticipated income sources during Renewalment. Your monthly income, or your Renewalment Paycheck, is a key financial focus during Renewalment.

In Renewalment, it's your monthly income (retirement paycheck) that's most important financially. Assets are obviously important, yet how your assets are positioned before retirement and then during retirement is what makes the most difference.

After my experience working as a professional in the financial services industry for three decades, as well as my reality of being two years into retirement when the COVID-19 pandemic hit, I believe the most critical years for investment income are the five years prior to and the five years immediately following retirement.

A little background…Over the last three decades I've been a financial advisor, a corporate executive, a leader of financial advisors, and a coach with financial advisors. My focus has been on personal and business leadership, helping people develop a healthy and confident relationship with money on a rock-solid biblical foundation, and thriving in Renewalment.

Helping people thrive in Renewalment includes the mutual development of a dynamic planning pathway. This pathway guides individuals and families in finding clarity of their unique and healthy retirement perspectives, personal and spousal identity, their core values, their unique purpose(s), their life dimension priorities, and a daily/weekly structure to live into their life, along with a "stress-free" Renewalment income plan.

This planning, especially the repositioning of your assets, is best if started during the five years prior to Renewalment. This allows you to best align with your "stress-free" retirement income plan. However, it's never too late. In retirement, it is all about income (your "retirement paycheck"), where your assets are invested (the type of assets more than specific investments), and avoiding the downside or negative order of returns.

Spending Plan

Before we dig into the first five years post-Renewalment, it's important to take a look at your Spending Plan. For many, the word "budget" has taken on a negative tone, as if the intent of a budget is to take some level of freedom away from you. In reality, a budget (I prefer "spending plan"), should be designed to give you a prioritized and intentional plan for spending freedom aligned with your life priorities. Such a plan, with spousal unity, is a key part of financial success and freedom.

You can call it what you want, but the critical step is to ensure you have a Spending Plan or budget aligned with your desired lifestyle. I also suggest a plan structured by the five keyways you use money: charitable giving, savings, taxes, debt, and lifestyle. Your spending plan must also have built-in financial margin so little changes don't upset your plan. Our tendency is to mainly focus on the income side. While the income side is obviously important, the expense side is equally important during retirement. You need to know and monitor where you're spending your money to align with your priorities and values and to thrive financially. This ensures you will have financial freedom.

It's helpful to think about which items in your spending plan are "fixed" month-to-month (e.g. groceries, utilities, gasoline, etc.) or quarter-to-quarter (e.g. homeowner dues, real estate taxes, etc.), as well as items that will most likely happen during the year, but the timing is unknown. These are items or bills that must be paid, and thus accounted for in your spending plan.

It's important to plan with flexibility in mind. We often have expenses that accumulate based on various situations that happen in life. You might find yourself planning an unexpected vacation, buying a car, remodeling a room, or in need of a new appliance. In those situations, you'll need to decide how to handle those unexpected expenses in relation to your spending plan.

Take the time now to document your current spending plan. For now, it might be a "spend what you want or when you need to" plan. However, it's time to become intentional about your spending plan and to identify where your hard earned dollars are currently being spent and invested. This will also help you identify what your desired retirement paycheck level is before you can identify what you deem "enough" for your asset accumulation. Warning: don't get bogged down attempting to narrow this down to the penny. It's best to simply determine a reasonable range. Having this clarity will greatly reduce stress levels when the traditional paychecks stop.

Review your spending plan at least once quarterly as it will need to be adjusted accordingly due to changes in life. Personally, I prefer to review our spending plan monthly since potential changes are usually smaller in nature and easier to account for on a monthly basis.

On a larger scale, most people also experience the so-called "go-go years," the "slow-go years," and the "no-go years." While the terminology may not be exact, research and experience suggests you'll tend to desire a larger spending plan in your earlier retirement years when you are healthier and want to be on the go compared to later retirement years when you may be comfortable spending more time at home.

If you haven't already started, begin eliminating your debt, including your mortgage. *True financial freedom going into Renewalment comes with having no debt in your spending plan during Renewalment.* The absence of debt gives you the freedom to make financial and emotional choices. Being free of debt has provided Bonnie and me a relatively stress-free financial mindset in Renewalment. Stuff will happen, but we know that being debt free offers us more financial choices. We have more options being debt free, and most importantly, rest on the foundation of knowing God's promises to provide for us.

The approach and mindset you take while developing and living your spending plan is important. A key problem is the way most of us - either intentionally or by default - prioritize where or how we spend our money. The tendency is to first use our money to fund our lifestyle, then to pay down what we owe (debt and taxes). Perhaps we will save some if there is anything left, but there is rarely anything left to give. According to biblical principles, the paradoxical way to prioritize is to first give. Then set aside savings (grow), pay down what you owe (debt and taxes), and finally, spend the remainder on your lifestyle. When aligned with your values and priorities, there will be enough to live on. Do you find it scary to consider this type of spending prioritization, versus the cultural approach? I get it! We also found it scary. It will take a leap of faith to truly trust God with your finances, but I can tell you from personal experience that it works.

The appendix has an example spending plan aligned with the five ways you spend money. Make it your own in unity with your spouse – then use it, be intentional and consistent, along with giving yourself grace. You will mess up, and that's okay. Learn, adjust, and move forward in harmony. It does not need to be perfect, as long as you focus on intentionally making positive progress.

In addition, when it comes to prioritizing debt repayment and savings/investment priorities, the previously outlined Investment Pyramid outlines a path to help you prioritize where and when you invest your dollars. It also includes the "why" for investing your dollars in the suggested order.

> *Keep your lives free from the love of money and be content with what you have, because God has said, "Never will I leave you; never will I forsake you." So we say with confidence, "The Lord is my helper; I will not be afraid. What can mere mortals do to me?"* (Hebrews 13:5-6 NIV)

The First Five Years Post-Renewalment

One of the key investment risks during the first five years in Renewalment is something called "order of returns". Sometime during your Renewalment years there will be a downturn in stock market returns. The concern is whether or not the market decline is early in Renewalment, mid-way through, or near the end of your Renewalment years. Over a twenty- or thirty-year period the average investment return, regardless of when the downturn(s) is, can be the same. Yet someone with significant negative returns in the later years of Renewalment will be in a much better position than someone with significant negative returns early in Renewalment, all else being equal. To help ensure you have the assets to generate income, the average return on your investments is important, but is less important than the order of the returns. The problem is that you can't predict the future – you don't know when the order of returns will help you or when it will hurt you.

A significant decline in the investment markets during the first five years of retirement can devastate your retirement assets and your probability of financial success in retirement, thus magnifying any anxiety you have of outliving your assets. That doesn't even take into consideration other issues like health care costs, long term care costs, or inflation. The good news is, you can plan for life's potential derailers, both known and unknown.

As of this writing, Bonnie and I are over four years into Renewalment, and we're in that critical five-years-post-retirement stage. It is not the best time for the COVID-19 pandemic, the closing of our economy, and significant stock market volatility. **If we had not planned for the potential of a negative order of returns, recent events could have devastated our retirement plans from a financial perspective and an emotional perspective.** So, why aren't we concerned, anxious, and fearful?

1. We have faith that God will provide for our needs.
2. We have a positive and grateful mindset and perspective.
3. Our retirement paycheck plan was built to weather the negative order of returns risk.

Our retirement income plan is based on clarity of the issues mentioned above, including an answer to "how much is enough" to provide for our family *and* our giving plan. We worked with our professional Christian financial advisors (CKA) prior to and during Renewalment to align assets with our desired monthly income for different timeframes and to address different potential investment risks. To do this, from a high-level perspective, we developed a "five buckets" approach – (1) Defense, (2) Defense and Offense, (3) Offense, (4) Derailers, and (5) Wealth Transfer.

1. **Defense** – a short-term bucket. At a time when investment returns were soaring higher and higher, we aligned some of the assets into very safe and conservative vehicles designed to generate a monthly paycheck for the first few years, regardless of what happens in the stock market or other outside influences. Greed says to keep all the dollars in the market since the return was higher…a lot higher at the time. Yet if we hadn't made this alignment, we would be in big trouble now with the onset of COVID-19, the economy shutting down, and the impact on the stock market. Had we not designed this "defense bucket" of assets to generate our monthly retirement paychecks without taking money from market investments, we might not be fearless. This first bucket helped us take the order of returns risk off the table during the early years of Renewalment. In addition to planning where to invest retirement assets for this period, this bucket also includes a personalized plan to maximize social security and pension benefits, along with other sources of passive income (e.g. rental income).

2. **Defense and Offense** – a medium-term bucket. Assets are invested in vehicles that allow us to play defense, to have down-side governors built in, and also provide for modest upside potential. Over time, these assets can be used to refill the short-term bucket.

3. **Offense** – a long-term bucket. Assets are more aggressively invested (e.g. in equity markets) with a long-term perspective. A long-term asset growth perspective for offense (for growth), helps address inflation risk concerns.

Over time, growth is harvested to help refill the first two buckets.

4. **Life's Derailers** – One of the biggest risks of derailment during retirement is health care costs, including long term care expenses. You must have a plan to address these expenses. It's not a matter of if they will occur, but when. Work with a professional Christian financial advisor (CKA) to develop a plan that works for you. There is no "one size fits all" when it comes to your Renewalment income and paycheck.

5. **Wealth (more than money) Transfer and Legacy** – Yes, estate planning, which is largely tax planning, for the transfer of assets to future generations is important. Yet, of far more importance is the transfer of your values, principles, insights, experiences, and how you were blessed with the assets and possessions you steward. Have a plan for transferring your "wealth" to children, grandchildren, nieces, nephews, and your favorite charitable organizations. My suggestion is that you start the transfer of your wealth while you're alive, ensuring the transfer of values and principles with your wealth. The transfer of wealth without the appropriate values and principles can harm the beneficiary more than it helps them.

A dynamic plan (one we can adjust as life changes), along with our faith, is why we're not worried about our financial future during Renewalment. We know we can and will thrive in Renewalment, even amidst challenges like the COVID-19 pandemic, economic shut-down, or anything else in the years to come.

A large part of our peace of mind comes from working with our Christian Financial Advisor (CKA) who guided the design of our plan, stress-tested the plan, probability-tested the plan, and is now executing the plan and updating it based on the changing environment and new learnings. We can then focus on thriving in Renewalment and not spend wasted time watching financial markets. We can focus on and enjoy our life's priorities.

Having our plan in place doesn't give us financial security, because only God can provide security. It does, however, help provide financial freedom and positive choices for when life happens. Financial freedom can help you thrive in Renewalment with provision, contentment, enjoyment, and a life of fulfillment. It will help you make a difference on purpose – loving and serving God by loving and serving others, and yes, that includes yourself.

As noted earlier, the surest way to build financial wealth is to spend less than you earn and to save over a long period of time. In order to intentionally and consistently do this, you must have a spending plan for the household, developed and imple-mented in unity. A spending plan honors your identity, purpose, and priorities in life, thus helping you thrive in Renewalment.

Path Forward

Retirement Income

- Develop a Mindset shift from accumulation to consis-tency of your monthly retirement paycheck. Align your assets accordingly.

Spending Plan

- Gain clarity of your current Spending Plan and desired future Spending Plan (Spending Plan outline in Appendix).
- Work "Your 5S Journey to Financial Freedom" following the steps outlined below.

First Five Years Post-Retirement

- Protect yourself against the order of returns. For example, from a high-level perspective, develop a "five buckets" approach – (1) Defense, (2) Defense and Offense, (3) Offense, (4) Derailers, and (5) Wealth Transfer.

Your 5S Journey to Financial Freedom

Changing your spending habits to increase margin is the only way to meet long-term goals and align your heart and hope toward eternity. Margin is the key to moving along your 5S Journey.

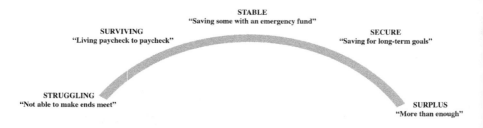

(5S Journey)

Where are you on your "5S Journey"?

How do you move from where you are to where you want to be? If you're content with where you are, how do you maintain that position?

It starts with the question, "In whom or what do you place your trust?" Will you trust God with your finances?

Without margin, it is difficult to respond to God's calling for your life and to meet the needs of those He has put in your life and entrusted to your care.

Building financial margin is the key to moving along the 5S Journey. Follow the steps outlined below for forward momentum.

Five Key Steps in Your 5S Journey

1. Develop routines for successful habits built on a rock-solid foundation of biblical principles and wisdom.
2. Create **margin** for the planned and the unplanned. Cash flow is critical.
3. Set Long-Term savings and investment goals.
4. Eliminate all debt and clarify legacy.
5. Give generously throughout the other four steps.

Moving from Struggling and Surviving to Stable...

1. Develop routines for successful habits built on a rock-solid foundation of biblical principles and wisdom.

Renewalment - Thriving in Retirement

a. Behavior follows belief – document and live your key financial perspectives.

b. God owns it all! Develop a mindset focused on stewardship.

c. Commit to a lifestyle aligned with the five Wise Financial Principles.

d. Intentionally and consistently execute a Spending Plan.

e. Get your spending under control and live within your means. Spending less than you earn is the only way to create margin.

Moving from Stable to Secure…

2. Create margin for the planned and the unplanned circumstances. Cash flow is critical.

a. Eliminate all high-interest and short-term debt.

b. Create an emergency fund.

c. Save for major purchases (e.g. appliances, car, repairs, etc.)

d. Avoid the accumulation of additional debt.

e. Insure against as many key financial derailers as you can.

f. Build additional margin.

Moving from Secure to Surplus…

3. Set long-term savings and investment goals.

   a. As a family, identify and prioritize long-term goals (e.g. college, new home, retirement, etc.)

   b. Clarify what you want your legacy to be (more on this topic later).

   c. Diversify your investment dollars, which is the #1 success factor when investing is diversification.

   d. Align with a professional Christian Financial Advisor or a Certified Kingdom Advisor (CKA). The most critical investing issues are your behavior, your emotions, and your common biases.

From Surplus and beyond...

4. Eliminate all debt and clarify your legacy.

   a. The elimination of debt provides more margin for choice and financial freedom.

   b. The elimination of all debt, including mortgage, opens financial freedom for retirement and other potential options.

5. Give generously throughout and within every step.

   a. You cannot outgive God. (Luke 6:38; Malachi 3:10)

   b. An attitude of gratitude and generosity is a key component for thriving in Renewalment.

Your unique situation will determine how you move through these steps. Some will be easier than others, and some may even be a little painful. However, I know from personal experience and from guiding others through the steps that the process will work for you if you're willing to work the process. The intentional and consistent work - with flexibility - is worth the payoff!

Have a sense of urgency and be patient with yourself. It doesn't happen overnight and there will be setbacks. Don't get frustrated with the setbacks. Simply get back on the plan and continue to move forward.

Summary

Retirement Income

- You need to transition your mindset and your plan from a main focus on asset accumulation to income (your retirement paycheck).

Spending Plan

- Without a spending plan you can't identify your "enough" for asset accumulation.
- A spending plan aligns your spending with your goals, values, and priorities.
- A flexible spending plan frees you and helps you thrive in Renewalment.
- The Investment Pyramid helps you prioritize debt repayment and savings/investment priorities. It outlines a path to help you prioritize, along with determining the "why" to invest your dollars in this order.

First five Years Post-Retirement

- Rearrange your assets for your defense, defense & offense, and offense assets to align with your priorities while planning for life's derailers and wealth transfer/legacy.

Chapter 6
SEVEN DIMENSIONS OF LIFE (LIFE PRIORITIES)

If you've been addressing the questions and the exercises up to this point, you at least have a starting point for gaining:

- clarity of your heart-felt beliefs and perspectives.
- clarity of your identity, including who you are and who you would like to be.
- clarity of your three to five core life values.
- clarity of your purpose: making a difference that matters and determining how you plan to pursue life in this season.
- clarity of what is "enough of a paycheck" for your Renewalment.

The next step is to gain clarity of your most valued life priorities. In order to truly thrive, your beliefs and your priorities need to be aligned with your behavior. Gaining clarity of your long-term priorities will also help you align your short-term disciplines, routines, and behavior. As mentioned previously, some

107

form of flexible structure will also be critical. (We'll discuss structure in the next section.)

We all have our own unique identity, core values, and purpose. The following are a few examples of my own personal life priorities:

- Some of my core heart-felt beliefs for Renewalment are:

  o God owns it all.
  o I'm a steward of what God has entrusted to my care.
  o Renewalment is a blend of vocation, service, and rest, not a life of leisure.
  o I am present and available to God and family.
  o I am busy on purpose with a purpose, and not in a hurry.

- My identity is as a child of God, and an heir with Jesus.
- My purpose is to be loved by God. My response is to love God and others, to "plant and water" Kingdom seeds, nurturing those entrusted to my care.
- My mission (why I exist) is to help others connect with Jesus and live into a 24/7 Christ-like lifestyle.
- My core values are to love, to serve, and to grow. I am to *love* God and my neighbor, to *serve* others by acting like Jesus, and to continually *mature* as a Jesus follower.
- My vision is for a church of unity based on the love of Christ. It is one that fully nurtures those entrusted to their care and unites the world.
- My goal is to be present in the now, to listen to God, to trust God, and to obey God. I want to nurture those

entrusted to my care at the moment, and to become more like Jesus.

This clarity has been critical in helping me thrive in Renewalment with gaining understanding of what really matters: alignment, focus, unity, decision-making, clarity of vocation/calling. I want to focus on fully serving those God has entrusted to my care, helping them live into a 24/7 Christ-like lifestyle aligned with their priorities on a rock-solid foundation of biblical principles.

The key to excelling in all aspects of your life (especially at work and in life) is found in your daily habits. Habits are driven by your identity, core values, purpose, and your life priorities.

Your daily habits will always trump your intentions and goals.

You may be asking something like, "What areas should I build my priorities around?" I'm so glad you asked. Edward Jones and Age Wave teamed up on a "comprehensive five-generation study including a survey of 9,000 adults in the U.S. and Canada." In this study they sought "to more deeply understand the retirement-related hopes, dreams and fears of our clients, their families and our communities."

They published the results of their study in a document called *The Four Pillars of the New Retirement*[1] and found that people who flourish after they retire will have built their lives on these four pillars: Health, Family, Purpose, and Finances. These are obviously four excellent pillars you could build your priorities on and around.

In my Life Coaching business, I help people gain clarity of their priorities through the lens of Seven Life Dimensions. In this section, I'll outline the seven dimensions along with a few questions and a format to help you identify your priorities in each of the seven areas. Remember, it's your Renewalment and your life, so you should identify the key areas and pillars that are most appropriate for you. I suggest you don't expand beyond seven dimensions. We can't assimilate more than seven, but feel free to combine and thus reduce the number based on your unique situation and beliefs.

I help people focus on these seven areas, with God woven in, through, and around each of them:

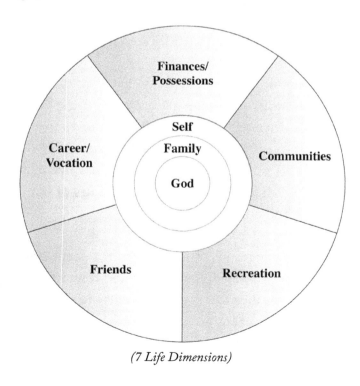

(7 Life Dimensions)

The primary objective is to develop a plan for a more vibrant life that will encompass your prioritized life dimensions while ensuring that God is woven in and throughout – knowing, loving, and serving God.

The secondary objective is to bring focus and prioritization to each of these seven life dimensions:

1. Self
2. Family
3. Career/Vocation
4. Finances
5. Friends
6. Community
7. Recreation

Clarify your Life Dimensions

What are the key life dimensions, or pillars, you plan to focus on setting priorities for? Write them down.

The following outlines the steps you can take to help you clarify your priorities for each of the life dimensions and then narrow the focus to your overall priorities. This exercise can be done at various times over the next month, quarter, or calendar year.

No matter how you choose to group your life dimensions, work through the following steps and answer the outlined questions.

Clarify Your Current State

For each life dimension…

1. Write down the three to five phrases that best describe your current reality with that dimension. Be truly honest with yourself, because it's critical to your success.
2. Write down one to five words, phrases, or sentences that pop into your mind (your initial thoughts – don't overthink it). Answer the following questions with the seven life dimensions in mind:

   a. What is right? (areas you want to optimize)
   b. What is wrong? (areas you may want to change)
   c. What is confusing? (areas you may need to clarify)
   d. What is missing? (areas you may want to add)
3. What has God put on your heart?
   a. What do you care most about?
   b. What do you dream about?
   c. How do you hope others describe you?
   d. Do your calendar and checkbook align/agree?

4. What activities are your biggest points of invigoration? What activities are the biggest drains to your energy?
5. What are your top three to five strengths? What are your top one to three passions?
6. Based on what you know today, what does "life success" look and feel like for you and your family? (Write down a few sentences or a few bullet points.)

Clarify Your Desired State

1. The Three Kinder Questions[2]: Life Planning (George Kinder)

The ultimate commodity that we are seeking is not money. It is time. Specifically, time to live the life that we find purposeful, productive, fulfilling, and satisfying.

   a. Question 1: Design your life

"Imagine that you are financially secure, and that you have enough money to take care of your needs, now and in the future. The question is, how would you live your life? What would you do with the money? Would you change anything? Let yourself go. Don't hold back your dreams. Describe a life that is complete and richly yours."

Of course, the purpose of the first Kinder question is to figure out what matters to you in life.

   b. Question 2: You have less time

"This time, you visit your doctor who tells you that you have five to ten years left to live. The good part is that you won't ever feel sick. The bad news is that you will have no notice of the moment of your death. What will you do in the time you have remaining to live? Will you change your life, and how will you do it?"

What if life sped the clock up? You had a plan to reach financial independence in 12 years, but now you only have 5 to 10 years left on this earth. How does this change things for you?

c. Question 3: Today's the day

"This time, your doctor shocks you with the news that you have only one day left to live. Notice what feelings arise as you confront your very real mortality. Ask yourself: What dreams will be left unfulfilled? What do I wish I had finished or had been? What do I wish I had done? [Did I miss anything]?"

2. Are your priorities in line with your life plan? Is your time reflective of what you care about? What do your financial habits reveal about your values? What "bucket list items" have you missed?
3. If today was your last day, what have you left unfinished? Of those things, what would bother you the most?
4. My life goal is…

For each life dimension…

5. Write down the three to five phrases or sentences that best describe your "desired state" for each of the life dimensions. Be fully honest with yourself.

Closing the Gap from Current State to Desired State

Take the time to review what you've drafted as your identity, your core values, your purpose(s), and the culture/environment that best fits you. The following twelve exercises will require significant attention and thoughtfulness. It might be helpful to take one step at a time and record your answers in a journal.

1. Review your responses to "Current State" question one and "Desired State" question five. Write a statement that defines the gap between your current and desired state for each of the seven life dimensions as you see it. Be honest with yourself. (Gap clarity.)

2. For each dimension, quickly jot down one to three things you could do to begin closing the gap between your current and desired states. (Gap closure ideation.)

3. Review your responses to "Current State" questions two – five, and your response to "Desired State" question one(a). Is there a gap? Use your insights to refine your responses to question two (Gap closure ideation).

4. Review your responses to "Current State" questions six and "Desired State" question one(b) and one(c). Is there a gap? Use your insights to refine your responses to question two (Gap ideation).

5. Review the gap areas you identified for each life dimension and in general, and rank the seven life dimensions from highest to lowest (one through seven) in priority of importance for closing the gap. Each dimension is important, yet closing the gap for some will have a higher priority currently. The order will most likely change in the future. Yet without a clear focus on the most important, none of them tend to be addressed. You need to be intentionally flexible.

6. Does the priority ranking you did in the prior step align with your life priorities? You might choose to combine some of the dimensions in your unique way.

7. For each life dimension, narrow down the steps you can take to start to close the gap between your "Current State" and "Desired State" to one, two, or three in

priority order. Will completion of these tasks progressively move you closer to your life goals and to living a fulfilling life of provision, contentment, and enjoyment? If yes, move forward and learn. If no, revisit steps one – six.

8. For each of the potential gap closure activities you identified in the prior step, note if your current desire is to focus on that activity, at least to start the activity, within the thirty days, sixty days, ninety days, twelve months, or longer. Remember to keep the priority for closing the particular life dimension into account.

9. List gap closure activities to focus on for the next thirty days.

10. List gap closure activities to focus on the next thirty-one to ninety days.

11. List gap closure activities to focus on the next ninety-one+ days.

12. If Jesus was living your life, how would He be prioritizing your gap closure? Do you need to change your priority list?

You have now taken your divergent ideation of gaps and potential gap closure steps, worked through convergent decision-making, and focused prioritization of how to approach closing the gaps at your own pace during Renewalment. This will give you a picture of how you can thrive in Renewalment based on your life priorities, not someone else's.

This will serve to help you to be busy on purpose with purpose, daily plant seeds for God's kingdom, not be in a hurry, and truly live through your identity and purpose, becoming the person you desire to be.

Next Steps

- Identify and document the key life dimensions you plan to focus on and set priorities for.
- Take the time now to work through the above steps. You can also find the steps outlined in the appendix.

You now have your next thirty-, sixty-, and ninety-day priorities drafted. Now you need a flexible weekly structure and rhythm to intentionally and consistently work the routines that will facilitate living your Desired State, allowing you to thrive in Renewalment.

Summary

- To live intentionally, to live the life you will be happy with, you must have clarity of your life priorities.

Chapter 7

LIVING A 24/7 CHRIST-LIKE LIFESTYLE RHYTHM

"You have two choices about who your ultimate authority will be: the world or God's Word—what other people say or what God says. If you base your decisions on current popular opinion, you'll always be on shaky ground because culture changes every day. On the other hand, if you base your decisions on God's Word, you'll have a solid foundation because his truth never changes." – Rick Warren

So, WHAT DO you plan to do with all of this material? Our natural tendency is to do nothing, to make no change, or to stay with the status quo, even when we know change is good for us and necessary. We need to be intentional about change and moving forward.

Intentionally striving to live a 24/7 Christ-like lifestyle – at church, at home, at work, out with friends, in the community, when no one is looking – will not just naturally happen. If we're honest, our natural tendency is to take the path of least resistance and go with the ways of the world around us. Yet we're called to be a light for the world, and to be a Christ-like example. We'll never be perfect, but we can live in such a way that people who know us will truly see that we listen to God, trust God, and obey God as we apply His teachings.

In order for this to happen, we need to be intentional and consistent. The only way to be intentional and consistent in striving to live as a 24/7 Christian is to create the structure that helps us build the desired habits into our daily life and routines. Reflecting back on the habits loop outlined in chapter three, we need to understand our cues and develop routines in our structure to create and reinforce the desired habits for living a 24/7 Christ-like lifestyle. Create a structure that fits your unique personality, behaviors, and desires.

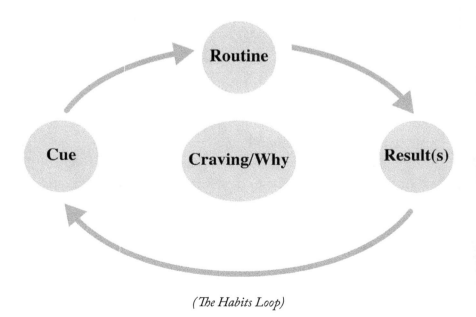

(The Habits Loop)

Structure for Change

Does the word "structure" make the hair on the back of your neck stand up? It does for many people. Common reactions include, "I'm seeking freedom" or "I'm looking to be myself." The paradox, however, is that structure is a pathway to facilitate freedom, margin, and living into your definition of success. Without structure, you'll bounce back and forth rather haphazardly and either lose your freedom or never find it at all.

Freedom = Discipline + Process + Structure

A lack of structure, or a "go-with-the-flow" approach to life in Renewalment, means you'll be 100 percent at the mercy of outside events and people. There are several external factors we cannot control, yet the path to being focused on your priorities and what's important to you and your family is manageable through structure. Don't just create structure for the sake of structure, but because it aligns with your values, principles, goals, and lifestyle. Structure should be aligned to help you intentionally and consistently live into your heart issues (perspective), identity, core values, purpose, and Renewalment paycheck. You need a structure with clear guideposts, yet with flexibility and choice. This ensures you can easily adjust to changes in your life, your life transitions, and those truly uncontrollable events. Most importantly, a structure gives you the flexibility and option to follow the path where God is calling you, and creates a margin for you to make a positive difference and impact for God's Kingdom.

Deciding to live a Christian lifestyle requires not just strictly learning the right words, but learning how to embody a way of life. Once you have a God-aligned perspective and clarity of your identity, values, purpose, and life goals, a structure that works for you is the path to thriving in Renewalment. Remember, it's your structure and your plan. You can change it when something isn't working or if life circumstances change. Be intentional, yet flexible.

> *"Your choices are far more powerful than your circumstances. You can see that clearly on how you spend your time. You may not like how complicated and busy your life has become. But with few exceptions, no one is forcing you to keep your life complicated"[1].* – Rick Warren

Rhythm Week

"Jesus lived in a particular rhythm of life that was essential to his well-being, his own faith-life, and his ministry to others. He had a way of life with his Father, his holiness, and wholeness. As a human being he proved he is the unique Son of God by living in continual and perfect oneness with the Father.

When we appreciate Jesus' rhythm of life and participate in it by relying on his Spirit of Grace it changes everything about our life." – Bill Gaultiere[2]

The general rhythm of Jesus' daily life included time with His Father in prayer, daily work (teaching, healing, performing miracles, developing disciples), spending frequent time in community, and rest. This included Sabbath rest weekly and a pause to create margin throughout the day.

The rhythm of Jesus' life seems like a good rhythm for us to follow, tweaked for the unique circumstances you may have. Creating your daily rhythm isn't easy and takes time and support. As with all parts of Renewalment, spousal unity and support is important, along with having the flexibility and uniqueness for you as an individual to live within a community.

The following is an example of what a typical rhythm day might look like:

Win the Morning:

It's important to start the day with positive energy and perspective.

- Devotions, Bible reading, and prayers
- Fitness: cardio, strength, stretching and balance (functional fitness)
- Breakfast
- Living out your vocation priorities for the day (paid or unpaid)
- Focus on the most important life priorities first

Enjoy the Day:

Enjoy life as it happens, knowing that your top priorities are being addressed.

- Lunch and community or alone time
- Living out your vocation (paid or unpaid)
- Giving back – service to/for others

- Living in community
- Busy on purpose, with purpose, but not in a hurry

End the Day & Recharge:

Have clear rituals to mark the end of your work day. We are not created to be workaholics.

Evening:

- Dinner
- Community
- Reading, games, etc.
- Relaxing
- Preparing for a great night of sleep

Perhaps a simpler approach to starting the discipline of a Rhythm Week is to divide each day into three sections: morning, afternoon, and evening. Include both priority and purely fun items in each section. This allows you to start small and work into your unique rhythm week over time. Remember to include time to relax, play, rest, and recharge throughout the remainder of your day.

Priorities and Life Dimensions

We are not called to retire from life. We are created to bear fruit. Being fruitful is not merely an option or suggestion...it is a calling. We were created to bear fruit (Genesis 1:28) and God is glorified when we 'bear much fruit' (John 15:8). We are called to serve God by serving others for our *entire life*. What this looks like may change over time, yet in order to live fruitful lives, we need to be intentional, consistent, and flexible as we live into God's will for our lives.

Just as a tangible example, following the process outlined in this book, my current Renewalment focus is three-fold: God, family, and vocation/service.

1. God – intentional daily time with God (daily devotions, Bible reading and prayer, and striving to live a Christ-like lifestyle in all aspects of my life.
2. Family – intentionally being present and available to help out, teach, and coach. This includes my own physical health routine of cardio, strength, balance, and stretching so I can be healthy and available.
3. Vocation/Service – to fully serve those God has entrusted to my care, and to help them live into a 24/7 Christ-like lifestyle as they mature as followers of Jesus. I place an emphasis on three areas:

   - Volunteer work
   - No Fear Consulting, LLC (a life-coaching and Renewalment-coaching business)
   - Writing this book as well as aligned articles and series for small groups
     … Living a fulfilling life of provision, contentment, and enjoyment.

I have clear priorities for each of the seven life dimensions. These are my life priorities, not intended to be anyone else's priorities. So merely as an example, mine are outlined in the appendix. Within these overarching life priorities, the above three are my current top focus areas. I weave others in as appropriate throughout my Rhythm Week.

Bonnie has her own version of her life priorities, unique to her (e.g. she is heavily engaged in the LCC K9 Comfort Dog ministry locally and nationally), and we're both aligned through our Christian perspectives, principles, values, goals, and dreams. We tend to be interdependently independent on a rock-solid foundation of Christ.

My planning starts long-term, as in "eternally" long term. Where do I want to be for eternity? Then, I bring a three-year window into focus. Based on my eternal goals, what might the next three years look like for me? Next, I focus on the immediate twelve-month window in front of me. Then I look at the next ninety days. From there, I can create a thirty-day action plan. This leads me to building a Rhythm Week for executing and implementing these goals into my life. I tend to preview the next thirty days and then get more detailed with a review of the prior week and a preview or planning for the week ahead on Friday or Saturday mornings. You can find the time that works best for you. I always pencil in this process since priorities can change and life brings unexpected events. I want the flexibility to adjust and remember to always build margin into my week for when life comes at me, while staying focused on my life priorities. Spending time on priorities is truly important to me as I live out the calling God has given me to the best of my abilities, and beyond, with the guidance of the Holy Spirit. When blocking time on my calendar to accommodate my priorities, I generally:

1. Ensure time with God is on the calendar. It's too easy to get busy and not take the time to include the most important thing on the calendar.
2. Ensure Sabbath rest time one day a week, as well as shorter times throughout each day.
3. Ensure that prioritized family time or events are on the calendar. This includes a monthly date day ("Yes Day") with Bonnie.
4. Ensure any meeting times I've already prioritized and committed to are on the calendar.
5. Ensure I have built-in time for margin.
6. Block time to work on any projects I set as a priority for the week ahead (e.g. time to prepare for appointments, write, read, coach, and think.)
7. Block time for things I see as fun or relaxing.

I suggest the following for a general weekly flow:

1. Review the past week and preview the "Weekly Priority Areas." Identify what you want to focus on during the week for each priority area.
2. Pipeline Movement – note the one, two , or three impact areas you want to move forward with during the week.
3. Ensure any critical family time (engagement with your family) or other appointments are time-blocked during the week.
4. Allocate the activities from steps one and two to a particular day(s) of the week to focus on them, limiting the volume of activity for any given day to one, two, or three key tasks.

5. Block time during the appropriate day to focus on the key activities identified in step four and to ensure margin time for flexibility as life happens (in pencil ☺).
6. Be disciplined and focused on priorities (vs. urgent stuff); yet stay flexible to adjust to opportunities.
7. Have FUN! Relax and enjoy life!

NOTE: Only you can effectively manage your time to focus on priorities.

It's healthy to conduct a mini-review of your structure and planning process on a monthly basis. Ask yourself reflection and planning questions such as:

- What themes emerged this past month?
- What did and did not work?
- What did I learn?
- How can I apply what I learned in the next month?
- What needs to shift in my plan based on new information and circumstances?

And as I noted, I use a pencil for my calendar so I can adjust appropriately. I'm consistently looking to find my zone, and to adjust for my unique rhythm of vocation, rest, and service.

You will not live out each day exactly like you planned, but the more you live the process the closer you will get. It's like throwing darts at a dart board. You will not always hit the bullseye, but throwing more darts will increase your likelihood of hitting the target. It's easier to adjust a plan in motion than one you never started.

If you don't plan your days around *your* priorities, others will plan your day for you with their own priorities in mind. Structure is your friend! Without it, we lose our identity, values, purpose, direction, energy, health, and confidence over time.

Start each day by asking, "God, what would you have me do today? What is the most important thing I can do today? What is the thing I can do today that will have the biggest impact for tomorrow?" Listen to God, trust God, and obey God (act).

"Carve your name on hearts, not tombstones."[3] – Shannon Alder

Path Forward

- Live into your own unique Rhythm Week – follow the steps outlined above.
- Live your life priorities, not the priorities other people impose on you. Own your priorities!

Summary

Habits Loop

- To live a 24/7 Christ-like lifestyle you will need to change a few routines to develop the healthy habits you want to live into.

Structure

- Paradoxically, the path to freedom is clarity of priorities and structure.

- Freedom = Discipline + Process + Structure

Rhythm Week

- To change your routines, you need structure and a new rhythm that is intentionally consistent and flexible.
- Jesus lived a consistent daily rhythm, on purpose with purpose, yet never in a hurry.
- To sustain change, start and end each day with God.

The general flow of a day might look like...

Win the Morning

1. Start the day off right, using your energy to accomplish important tasks.
2. Focus on the highest priority areas in the morning.

Enjoy the Day

3. Do naturally invigorating activities along with a "must-do" item or two in the afternoon.
4. Be present for items as they come at you.

End the Day (ritual)

5. Review and Preview – let go of the unresolved issues of the day.
6. Be present, enjoy the evening, relax, and recharge.

Chapter 8

DYNAMIC PLANNING and ACTION

GOD DIDN'T GIVE you gifts just to use them for yourself. "Each of you should use whatever gift you have received to serve others, as faithful stewards of God's grace in its various forms." (1 Peter 4:10 NIV)

If you know what you're good at and you know that many people in the world probably need your help, what are you going to do about it? Who are you serving? Who are you going to help between now and when your story ends and eternity begins?

You need a plan in order to do what you ought to do and want to do. Your plan should be focused on doing the will of God, and growing the Kingdom in the process. God makes it clear in the Parable of the Talents (Matthew 25:14-30) that we are to be diligent stewards, overseeing the care and growth of what has been entrusted to us. Biblically we are not called to retirement, yet we are called to be faithful throughout our entire life. We might retire from a particular job and full-time compensation, yet we can't retire from service.

Our planning is not to be self-serving. We are to seek first the kingdom of God (Matthew 6:33), to put God first (Proverbs 3:6), and when we commit to the Lord in whatever we do, He will establish our plan (Proverbs 16:3).

Careful planning puts us ahead in the long run, while hurry and scurry (or just waiting for something to happen) will put us further behind (Proverbs 21:5). With wise counsel our plans will succeed (Proverbs 15:22). God has plans for us to prosper and to give us hope and a future (Jeremiah 29:11). God made you on purpose for a purpose. He has a plan for your life that only you can fulfill.

The question is will you listen to God, discerning His will for you? Will you trust God in all aspects of your life? Will you obey God and take action by faithfully taking the first step?

You are expected to plan and prepare as you align with God's path for you. You are not to stand around and expect things to happen. You're expected to take the first step, not to wait for the entire plan to be revealed to you. Trust God to reveal the first step, then act. Then trust God for each consecutive step and adjust in a dynamic, ongoing manner as you listen for God's guidance.

A word of caution: be careful to avoid the trap I got caught in. Rather than first discerning God's plan designed in advance for me, I found myself developing plans for doing good and helping others, and then inviting God to help me with *my* plans. From experience, I can assure you that God's plan works out better.

So, what is the will of God? According to Scott Cormode in his book *The Innovative Church*[4]:

> "The majority of Scripture makes clear what is the will of God. The will of God is to 'love the Lord your God with all your heart' and to 'love your neighbor as yourself'." The will of God is to "worship no other gods," to "honor father and mother," and to "remember the Sabbath day." The will of God is to "care for the widow, the orphan, and the alien in your midst." The will of God is to be generous with your money, especially toward the needy. The will of God is to "be poor in spirit," meek, and merciful—to be salt and light, and to turn the other cheek. That is what it means to "present your bodies as a living and holy sacrifice." That is what it means to "prove what is the will of God, what is good and acceptable, and perfect."

The will of God is more about what to do than what not to do. Love God. Love your neighbor. Be generous. In short, practice grace as your Savior practiced grace.

For freedom Christ has set us free. We are free to love God and love our neighbor in myriad ways.

Discernment begins with listening. Indeed, it involves four kinds of listening. It involves listening to God, listening to Scripture, listening in community, and listening to the people entrusted to our care. And when we do that, we have the freedom to act in any way that conforms to God's reconciling acts—that is, in any way so that we love God, love neighbor, care for the marginalized, and enact the Sermon on the Mount."

God's overall will (His "macro-purpose") for us is clear: love God, love others, and serve God by serving others, and striving to become more like Jesus. With this mindset woven in and through all we do, our day-to-day vocation and calling is wide open. You were made on purpose for a purpose. God has a plan for your entire life. To help discover your vocation, or how you plan to serve the Lord on a day-to-day basis, you need to listen. Listen to God, scripture, those you trust in your community, and to those entrusted to your care.

God has an overarching goal for each believer to become more like Jesus. He also has an individualized plan for each of us.

You can start each day asking, "God how do I best steward the resources (time, talent, experience, knowledge, relationships, finances, and people) you have entrusted to my care today?" Then comes the hard part: patiently listen, act, obey.

> "..*Blessed rather are those who hear the word of God and keep it!*" (Luke 11:28 ESV)

You must be intentional in keeping your plan dynamic. Have a true-north understanding of God's will for you (the why and what) and then adjust the how as you experience change in the world around you and with the people entrusted to your care.

A thought process that's been helpful to me as I strive to discern God's will for my life before and during Renewalment comes from guidance provided by Dr. Charles Stanley[5] (InTouch Ministries) in a sermon I watched, listened to, and relistened to on TV. It's key to find a quiet time free from all the outside noise, to ask the questions, to listen, read, and observe without a specific outcome in mind.

- How do you discern God's will for you?

  1. Go to the Word of God.
  2. Pray and listen.
  3. He will show you through your circumstances.
  4. Listen to Godly counsel. "In this situation, what do you think the word of God says?"
  5. God may use unusual manifestations.

  "This is the confidence we have in approaching God: that if we ask anything according to his will, he hears us. And if we know that he hears us—whatever we ask—we know that we have what we asked of him." (1 John 5:14-15 NIV)

- Hindrances to hearing God's will:

  1. Self will
  2. The influence of others
  3. Ignorance of God's word

4. Doubt
5. Feelings of unworthiness (God loves us)
6. Willful or known sin

- How do you know for sure it's God's will?

    1. Is this direction consistent with the Word of God?
    2. Can I honestly ask God to help me achieve this?
    3. Do I have genuine peace about my situation?
    4. Does this decision align with who I am as a follower of Jesus?
    5. Does this decision fit into God's overall plan for my life?
    6. If I make this decision, will it honor God?

Remember, it's not so much *what* you do for your vocation that matters, but *who* you do it *for. "Take your everyday, ordinary life – your sleeping, your eating, going-to-work, and walking around life – and place it before God as an offering."* Romans 12:1a (Message)

Will you be working for yourself or God in Renewalment?

Throughout every season of your life, your identity as a child of God will never change. Your purpose and passions might change over time. God's individual calling for you will most likely change as you grow and mature. But your true north needs to hold steady. Seek first the kingdom of God, and live out God's macro-calling for you. Be sure you are continually in communication with God (through prayer, God's Word, fellow Jesus followers, devotions, and reflection) in order to discern and implement your day-to-day lifestyle through your

136

personalized Rhythm Week. Discernment is not so much a singular event as it is an ongoing conversation with God.

You are much more likely to get to where you want to get to if you have an intentional plan and structure to get there.

As you work your plans remember "Many are the plans in a person's heart, but it is the Lord's purpose that prevails" (Proverbs 19:21) and "Do not wear yourself out to get rich" (Proverbs 23:4). You'll want to build Sabbath rest into each and every day, not just one day of the week. You need margin in your days to ask, listen, think, reflect, and act. This will allow you to hear the quiet whispers of God, and to be flexible and available for your life priorities.

As previously mentioned, I'd suggest the "job to be done" is to be a great steward (remember, God owns it all) of all that God has entrusted to your care, including your relationships, networks, spiritual gifts, talents, resources, and finances. Live out God's plan for your life, and strive to be more like Jesus. As a result, you will be preparing for eternal life in heaven.

Regardless of the size of our decisions, God calls us to vigilance (keeping careful watch), prudence (showing care and thought for the future), and wisdom (practicing good judgement based on experience and knowledge). It goes without saying that the best choices you can make are those rooted in Biblical principles. While it's easy to write that on paper, it's much more challenging to live out in the playing field of daily execution. That's why you need to surround yourself with a group of like-minded peers, gaining insight and wisdom from other Christians who have been there. You can learn how to produce real and measured results while making God-honoring decisions, and holding each other mutually accountable.

As mentioned before, *we are not called to retire from life.* We are called to "bear fruit" (Genesis 1:28) our entire life, regardless of the changes we face in the midst of various life transitions. Retiring to a life of fruitlessness is not an option. God is glorified when we "bear much fruit" (John 15:8).

Experience also suggests there will be times when you will start down some dark rabbit-holes. You will face boredom, loss of identity, loss of purpose, and a variety of fears. Being in God's word through prayer and devotions is critical for catching yourself from going too deep into the rabbit-holes. We all have rabbit-holes, but the key is to catch ourselves when we start down one.

Quality relationships are also essential to this season of life. In his book *The Power of the Other*[6], Dr. Henry Cloud identifies the importance of what he calls Corner Four relationships. A Corner Four relationship is someone you trust and can be totally honest with, knowing they will not judge you, but will also hold you accountable.

> *"A real connection is one in which you can bring your whole self, the real, authentic you, a relationship to which you can bring your heart, mind, soul, and passion. Both parties in the relationship are wholly present, known, understood, and mutually invested.*

What each truly thinks, feels, believes, fears, and needs can be shared safely.

Corner Four is a place where people have true connection, where they can be authentic — not copied, not false or imitation, as Webster defines authentic. When you can find a place to be authentic, you can gain access to the resources that you have been wanting.

Corner Four accountability is a commitment to what is best at three levels: (1) both or all the individuals involved, (2) the relationship(s), (3) the outcomes. There are some big factors in this kind of accountability that keep it from going the route of shame and push it forward to greater performance: The first is the clarity of agreed-upon expectations, which have been communicated and embraced by all. Second, the timing of those expectations is early and continuous.

Great Corner Four relationships increase responsibility by preventing most surprises.

Stay current, whatever that means and however necessary. On the other hand, get out of each other's face as well.

People in Corner Four relationships care, are honest, and fix problems… caring enough about someone to not be hurtful in how we say things, the honesty to

*say them directly, and a focus on behavior change
and better results. Remember these three accountability aspects: the individual, the relationship, and
the outcomes."*

Be intentional about developing and nurturing a few Corner
Four relationships for your life, especially the spiritual, familial,
financial, and vocational dimensions of your life. Surround
yourself with people who fill you up, and run from people who
drain your energy.

What's your plan to succeed spiritually?

Remember, God has great plans for you. Listen. Trust. Obey.

*"For I know the plans I have for you," declares
the Lord, "plans to prosper you and not to harm
you, plans to give you hope and a future. Then you
will call on me and come and pray to me, and I will
listen to you."* (Jeremiah 29:11-12 NIV)

Path Forward

- Using the path outlined above, continuously be dis-
  cerning God's will for your life.
- Take the time now to clarify your life priorities (Seven
  Life Dimensions)

  => clarify your three to five-year goals
  => clarify your next twelve-month objectives
  => prioritize your next ninety-day priorities

=> prioritize your next rolling thirty-day priorities focus areas

=> execute through your Rhythm Week

Summary

Planning

- You need a plan in order to do what you ought to do and want to do. You need to intentionally and consistently work your plan. If you work your plan, your plan will work for you.
- God made you on purpose for a purpose. He has a plan for your entire life.
- We are not called to retire from life.

Discernment

- Discern God's plan for you and jump on board. Follow God's plan, not your plan for God.
- Ask the question, "Will I follow God's calling for me, and will I be obedient?"

Chapter 9
SOME CONCLUDING WORDS

THROUGH MY EXPERIENCE with learning to thrive in this new phase called Renewalment, I have discovered the importance of seeking clarity and purpose when faced with a life transition. It is essential to prayerfully and intentionally work towards establishing your identity and purpose in Renewalment. Determine three to five core values and use them to gain clarity of your income opportunities, a rhythm and structure for daily living, and intentional dynamic planning.

Key Steps:

Clarifying your core beliefs and perspectives.

Clarifying your identity (who you are or would like to become) and your core values.

Clarifying your core macro and micro-purpose(s) in life (how you plan to pursue life and where you find your energy and drive).

Identifying your life priorities through the lens of the Seven Life Dimensions.

Clarifying the income you need and desire in Renewalment, then identifying "How much is enough?"

Finding a structure & rhythm routine that provides the structure you'll need to intentionally and consistently live your life priorities to thrive in Renewalment.

Finding the ongoing accountability path through continuous Dynamic Planning, Core Relationships, and Mutual Accountability.

My suggestion is to find a trustworthy life-planning coach to help guide you through these steps. If you decide to work the process on your own, engage a trusted colleague to help hold you accountable and use the questions outlined in each chapter.

So, when do I start? **NOW!** No matter your age, you can start to prepare for this life transition and for other life transitions that occur before and after you officially enter Renewalment. If you start your preparation for Renewalment ahead of time, you have the opportunity to test out some of your ideas in advance.

If you're already in "retirement" and haven't prepared by following the above seven steps, I suggest you start with a Sabbatical pause. This includes a time of self-surrender (it's not about you), an intentional time of prayer and being in

144

the Word, fasting, reflection, and conversations with God and trusted Christian colleagues as you work through the seven steps. This time should also include intentional rest, relaxation, exercise, fitness, vacation, and time to unplug.

I've also learned you will all mess up along the way. You will likely fall back into poor habits, so you must have a process to catch yourself. Develop a plan to help you work through issues like boredom, unique fears, and going down other rabbit holes. Be certain this plan is built on a rock-solid foundation of Biblical principles. Anything else is shifting sand and you'll continue down an unpredictable and unstable path.

You'll need clarity of your heart-felt beliefs, identity, core values, purpose, personal self-care approach, most valued priorities, "enough of a paycheck," *and* a simple and flexible structure to thrive in Renewalment intentionally and consistently (not perfectly). This is a path toward living a joy-filled life of provision, contentment, generosity, and enjoyment.

As of this writing, Bonnie and I have been in Renewalment a little over four years. We have gone through all the normal ups and downs of life. Thankfully, the lows have been manageable, and we either caught ourselves or had planned for them. The highs have been pure enjoyment since we have a biblical foundation for our plan. As a result, it's easy to get back on track knowing the foundational principles are transcending, always true, and never changing.

I've heard it said, *"The only parts of the Bible you truly believe are the parts you put into practice. If what you say you believe doesn't change how you live your life, then you probably don't really believe it."*

Do you believe what the Bible says is the truth or not?

Will you intentionally attempt to live your life and your Renewalment guided by biblical truth or not?

It's your choice. It's also a choice whether or not you'll thrive in Renewalment by living an external life (behavior and actions) congruent with your internal life (values and beliefs) or not.

As we learn in 1 Timothy, you can live a life of provision, contentment, and enjoyment! This is achieved by loving God and your neighbor, serving God by serving your neighbor, and finding your own blend of service, rest, and vocation before and upon entering Renewalment.

START TODAY!

A plug:

I have a small consulting firm, No Fear Consulting, LLC. My focus is Life Coaching, Renewalment Coaching, and/or Financial Coaching for individuals and couples. As your coach, I become your conscience and guide as you intentionally walk through the processes to clarify your identity, core values, purpose, and life priorities. I help you live your life through the lens of your priorities versus, for example, living your life through a work lens. The goal is to help you excel in life, including in your work and vocation. My goal is to help you live a life of provision, contentment, and enjoyment.

If you'd like to learn more, email me at <u>brucefear7@gmail.com</u> and we will discuss the process, desired outcomes, as well as my modest fee.

APPENDIX

Key Support Tools/Documents Reference

- Five Wise Biblical Financial Principles - page 23-24
- Identity, Purpose, Core Values & Purpose Key Questions - page 54
- Your 5S Journey to Financial Freedom - page 60-62
- 7 Life Dimensions Process Steps - page 65-67
- Rhythm Week Process Steps - page 72-73
- Discernment Questions - page 76-77
- Key Steps - page 80
- Spending Plan - page 83-85

SPENDING PLAN: CASH FLOW/ MARGIN WORKSHEET

Date:

INCOME

	Monthly	Annual
Income/Salary	$_____	$_____
Dividends, interest, capital gains	$_____	$_____
Rent	$_____	$_____
Other Income	$_____	$_____
Social Security	$_____	$_____
Pension	$_____	$_____
Total Money In:	$_____	$_____

GIVE

	Monthly	Annual
Church	$ _____	$ _____
Charitable Organizations	$ _____	$ _____
Giving while alive	$ _____	$ _____
Other	$ _____	$ _____
Total Give:	$ _____	$ _____

OWE – DEBT

Mortgage	$ _____	$ _____
Home equity loan/line of credit	$ _____	$ _____
Automobile loans	$ _____	$ _____
Student loan payments	$ _____	$ _____
Credit card payments	$ _____	$ _____
Other debt	$ _____	$ _____
Total Debt:	$ _____	$ _____

OWE – TAXES

Property Taxes	$ _____	$ _____
Federal Income Tax	$ _____	$ _____
OASDI Taxes	$ _____	$ _____
Medicare Tax	$ _____	$ _____
State Income Tax	$ _____	$ _____
Other taxes	$ _____	$ _____
Total Taxes:	$ _____	$ _____

GROW

	Monthly	Annual
Emergency Fund	$ _____	$ _____
Retirement Savings	$ _____	$ _____
Other savings	$ _____	$ _____
Other savings	$ _____	$ _____
Total Grow:	$ _____	$ _____

LIVE

Housing and Maintenance

	Monthly	Annual
Rent	$ _____	$ _____
Homeowners/Renters Insurance	$ _____	$ _____
Utilities (gas, electric, sewer, garbage, etc.)	$ _____	$ _____
Maintenance/repair	$ _____	$ _____
Association Fees	$ _____	$ _____
Furniture, decorations, lawn, etc.	$ _____	$ _____
Other	$ _____	$ _____
Total Housing & Maintenance:	$ _____	$ _____

Transportation

Auto insurance premiums	$ _____	$ _____
Auto registration/taxes	$ _____	$ _____
Gasoline	$ _____	$ _____
Maintenance/Licenses	$ _____	$ _____
Public Transportation/Tolls	$ _____	$ _____
Transportation Total:	$ _____	$ _____

Health Care

Insurance premiums (medical, dental, vision, etc.)	$ _____	$ _____
Health Savings Account	$ _____	$ _____
Co-Pay/Out-of-pocket	$ _____	$ _____
Prescriptions	$ _____	$ _____
Other	$ _____	$ _____
Health Care Total:	$ _____	$ _____

Other Expenses	Monthly	Annual
Food/Groceries	$ _____	$ _____
Phone(s)	$ _____	$ _____

Internet/Television	$ _____	$ _____
Children (e.g. child support, daycare, activities, etc.)	$ _____	$ _____
Clothing/Personal Care	$ _____	$ _____
Education	$ _____	$ _____
Pets	$ _____	$ _____
Financial planning/legal/ tax accounting fees	$ _____	$ _____
Insurance Premiums (e.g. life, LTC, disability, etc.)	$ _____	$ _____
Vacations/Travel	$ _____	$ _____
Gifts/Holidays	$ _____	$ _____
Fun and Entertainment	$ _____	$ _____
Personal Allowances	$ _____	$ _____
Other	$ _____	$ _____
Total Other Expenses:	$ _____	$ _____

Total Live: $ _____ $ _____

Total Money In: $ _____ $ _____

Total Give + Owe Debt +
Owe Taxes + Grow + Live: $ _____ $ _____

Margin: $ _____ $ _____

NOTES

All scripture references are taken from Bible Gateway.

Bible Gateway. Bible Gateway/Zondervan, 2008. www.bible-gateway.com.

Introduction:

1. Warren, Rick. "Can You Trust God for Your Destiny?" Posted August 8, 2019. *Daily Hope with Rick Warren.* connect@news-letter.purposedriven.com.

Chapter 1

1. Garabato, Natalia. "Why Workers Retire When They Do: A Survey of U.S. Retirees." January 7, 2016.

2. Udo, Joe. "5 Common Reasons People Retire Early." Posted December 5, 20213. *U.S. News & World Report.*

https://money.usnews.com/money/blogs/on-retire-ment/2013/12/05/5-common-reasons-people-retire-early.

3. Osborne, John W. "Psychological Effects of the Transition to Retirement." *Canadian Journal of Counseling and Psychotherapy* 46, no. 1, ISSN 0826-3893 (2012): 45-48.

4. Sullivan, Dan, and Hamish MacDonald. *My Plan For Living to 156: Imaginatively extend your lifetime to transform how to live in the present.* Toronto, Canada: Author Academy Elite, 2018.

Chapter 2

1. Warren, Rick. "Can You Trust God for Your Destiny?" Posted August 8, 2019. *Daily Hope with Rick Warren (connect@newsletter.purposedriven.com).*

2. Graham, Billy. "5 Things the Bible Says About Work." Posted August 27, 2018. *BGEA Billy Graham Evangelistic Association.* https://billygraham.org.

3. Warren, Rick. "Your Gifts Are for Other People." Posted November 5, 2021. *Daily Hope with Rick Warren. (connect@newsletter.purposedriven.com)*

4. "What Should a Christ-Centered Life Look Like?" Accessed October 8. 2021. *Got Questions.* https://www.gotquestions.org/Christ-centered-life.html.

5. Veith, Gene Edward. "Martin Luther on Vocation and Serving Our Neighbor." March 20, 2016. *Working for Our Neighbor.* https://www.action.org.

6. Blue, Ron. Found of the Ronald Blue Company, Kingdom Advisors, and the Ron Blue Institute for Financial Planning. RBI/KA training event.

7. Blue, Ron. *Simplifying the Money Conversation.* Marion, Indiana: Ron Blue Institute, Ron Blue Library, 2018.

8. Blue, Ron. The Investment Pyramid has been adapted for professional use from a training session presented by Ron Blue. RBI/KA training event.

9. "What Does the Bible Say About Saving for Retirement?" Accessed December 7, 2021. *Got Questions.* https://www.gotquestions.org/saving-for-retirement.html.

10. Hawkins, O.S. *Antology Lessons from the Ant for our Financial Future.* Dallas: Guidestone, 2007. www.GuideStone.org.

11. Bentley, Chuck. "What Does the Bible Say About Retirement?" Posted October 4, 2017. *Crown Financial Ministries.* https://www.crown.org.

12. Buchanan, Mark. *The Rest of God: Restoring Your Soul by Restoring Sabbath.* Nashville: Thomas Nelson, 2006.

Chapter 3

1. Maxwell, John. "It All Comes Down to What You Do Daily." Posted January 14, 2015. https://www.johnmaxwell.com.

2. Duhigg, Charles. *The Power of Habit: Why We Do What We Do In Life and Business.* New York: Random House, 2012.

3. Buchanan, Mark. *The Rest of God: Restoring Your Soul by Restoring Sabbath.* Nashville: Thomas Nelson, 2006.

4. Blue, Ron. *Simplifying the Money Conversation.* Marion, Indiana: Ron Blue Institute, Ron Blue Library, 2018.

5. Jeremiah, David, Dr. "Contentment — When Enough Is Enough." *Turning Point with Dr. David Jeremiah.* https://www.oneplace.com.

6. Dungy, Tony and Nathan Whitaker. *The One Year UNCOMMON LIFE Daily Challenge.* Winter Park, Florida: Tyndale House Publishers, Inc., 2011.

7. Batterson, Mark. *Whisper: How to Hear the Voice of God.* New York: Multnomah, 2017.

8. "What is God's view of pleasure? Is He opposed to pleasure?" Copyright 2011-2012. *Compelling Truth | Christian Life.* https://www.compellingtruth.org.

Chapter 4

1. Earls, Aaron. "Where Americans Find Their Identity." Posted 2018. *American Views on Personal Identity and Disappointments.* LifewayResearch.com.

2. "8 Unhealthy Habits Aging Adults Should Quit." Posted September 20, 2017. *Homecare Assistance.* https://www.home-careassistanceplano.com/unhealthy-habits-seniors-should-quit.

3. "For Seniors, Unhealthy Living May Lead to Disability." Posted July 24, 2013. *MedicineNet.* https://www.medicinenet.com/script/main/art.asp?articlekey=171941.

4. Roberts, Mark D. "Purpose is Key to Third Third Flourishing." Posted January 6, 2021. *Fuller De Pree Center.* https://depree.org/purpose-is-key-to-third-third-flourishing/.

5. "Where Americans Find Meaning in Life." Posted November 20, 2018. *Pew Research Center*

Religion & Public Life. https://www.pewforum.org/2018/11/20/where-americans-find-meaning-in-life.

6. Kirby, Stephanie. "Inspirational Billy Graham Quotes About Faith." February 26, 2021. *Everyday Power.* https://everyday-power.com/billy-graham-quotes.

7. Warren, Rick. *The Purpose Driven Life: What on Earth am I Here For?* Grand Rapids: Zondervan, 2002.

8. Pemberton, Ryan. "Frederick Buechner on Calling: Your Deep Gladness & The World's Deep Hunger." Posted December 22, 2014. *Called the Journey.* http://www.calledthejourney.com/blog/2014/12/17/frederick-buechner-on-calling.

Chapter 6

1. "The Four Pillars of the New Retirement." June 2021. *Edward Jones.* https://www.edwardjones.com/sites/default/files/ acquiadam/2021-06/Four-Pillars-US-Report-June-2021.pdf.

2. Roth, J.D. "George Kinder: Three Questions About Life Planning." December 12, 2020. *Get Rich Slowly.* https://www.getrichslowly.org/ george-kinder-three-questions-about-life-planning/.

Chapter 7

1. Warren, Rick. "Your Choices Control Your Calendar." Posted July 13, 2021. *Daily Hope with Rick Warren.* connect@newsletter. purposedriven.com.

2. Gaultiere, Bill, Ph.D. *Your Best Life in Jesus' Easy Yoke: Rhythms of Grace to De-Stress and Live Empowered.* Irvine, CA: CreateSpace, 2016.

3. Alder, Shannon L. *Quotefancy.* https://quotefancy.com/ quote/28418/Shannon-L-Alder-Carve-your-name-on-hearts-not-tombstones-A-legacy-is-etched-into-the.

4. Cormode, Scott. *The Innovative Church: How Leaders and Their Congregations Can Adapt in an Ever-Changing World.* Grand Rapids, MI: Baker Academic, 2020.

5. Stanley, Charles, Dr. "He Will Show You His Will | Timeless Truths." *YouTube*, uploaded by In Touch Ministries, July 17, 2021, https://www.youtube.com/watch?v=_coYrXivn6Y.

6. Cloud, Henry, Dr. *The Power of Other: The Startling Effect Other People Have on You, From the Boardroom to the Bedroom and Beyond - and What to Do About It*. Harper Business, 2016.

CPSIA information can be obtained
at www.ICGtesting.com
Printed in the USA
BVHW092121071122
651017BV00006B/17

9 781662 848537